TRUST BUILDING WITH CHILDREN WHO HURT

A One-to-One Support Program For Children Ages 5 to 14

Ruth P. Arent, M.A., M.S.W.

THE CENTER FOR APPLIED
RESEARCH IN EDUCATION
West Nyack, New York 10995

Library of Congress Cataloging-in-Publication Data

Arent, Ruth P.
    Trust building with children who hurt: a one-to-one support
program for children ages 5 to 14 / Ruth P. Arent
        p.   cm.

    Includes bibliographical references (p.) and index.
    ISBN 0-87628-191-9
    1. Trust (Psychology) in children. 2. Adjustment
(Psychology) in children. 3. Children—Counseling
of. 4. School psychology.
I. Title.
BF723.T78A74 1992
371.4'6—dc20   91-23528
                                     CIP

ISBN 0-87628-191-9

**The Center for Applied
Research in Education**
Business Information & Publishing Division
West Nyack, NY 10995

Simon & Schuster, A Paramount Communications Company

PRINTED IN THE UNITED STATES OF AMERICA

About the Author

Ruth P. Arent received her B.A. degree from Skidmore College (Saratoga Springs, New York), her M.A. degree in Psychology/Child Development from the University of Iowa, and her M.S.W. from the University of Denver Graduate School of Social Work.

Ms. Arent has more than 35 years experience as an educational consultant leading workshops/inservice programs in such areas as child victims, children under stress, unmotivated students, and teacher stress and success; she currently teaches for several Colorado universities. She conducted a private therapy practice for many years and worked as a teacher and social worker in school systems.

Ms. Arent has written extensively for professional publications, including *Learning Magazine* and *Gifted Child Monthly*, and has authored numerous books and booklets in the field. She also travels extensively presenting professional seminars. Her book, *Stress and Your Child, A Parent's Guide to Symptoms, Strategies and Benefits* (Prentice-Hall, 1984) continues to be used as a text in parenting classes and as a reference for professionals and parents.

Acknowledgments

As a stalwart, patient, and helpful coworker, Berniece Antonio is a prize. Without her, this book might still be a bundle of ideas in search of expression and order. Bernie provides great feedback. She is a good friend and I am very grateful.

Indeed, many have been supportive during my struggle to finish this task. Special thanks to my family, and to Ruth Spar, Kathy Moorhead, Don Lorenz, and to the many counselors and teachers who have enthusiastically validated this Trust Building Program in their work with children.

Contents

The Importance of a Trust Building Program

Children Who Hurt are at risk of becoming Children Who Hate. Children Who Hurt and Children Who Hate are wonderful kids but something sad or bad has happened in their lives. They are anxious and frightened—some neglected, others abused. They have lost trust in adults; perhaps they never have experienced trust. Without a trusting relationship, they lose faith in themselves and become locked in self-defeating attitudes. They are damaged children who may become angry, antagonistic, withdrawn or defensive. They can become a real pain in the neck. They are predictably immature. Their inappropriate behaviors are pleas for unqualified acceptance as human beings—as children. These children hurt because they have low self-esteem and do not trust adults. Children Who Hate are severely damaged and must have long-term therapy. Children Who Hurt have sufficient strength to use short-term *one-to-one help* such as a Trust Building Program. Children Who Hurt may become Children Who Hate unless they learn to trust and their self-esteem improves. That's the message of this book. That's what a Trust Building Program can accomplish.

> ## One-to-one work is essential

Children Who Hurt still have sufficient ego to benefit from work with an adult—if the adult is available. Children will rarely ask for help; it is *not* to be expected. Their inappropriate actions are their pleas for help. Most *will* respond to the overtures of a caring adult. It is an aspect of their strength—their wellness. A Trust Building Program is designed to build on these strengths to create a powerful trust experience. Children Who Hurt can benefit from help to become more stable and self-accepting. *They need vivid encouragement*—wrapped in hope.

Many adults already do wonderful things for kids. They reach out in caring ways, but too often it is in a group or simply a random approach. In contrast, the Trust Building Program described in this book is orderly and will help repair a child's trust and instill confidence through a series of fourteen to twenty planned biweekly one-to-one meetings. It is asking too much of a Child Who Hurts to pull together all the pieces needed to instill confidence and repair trust from group interactions or counselor groups. The pieces and continuity must come from a one-to-one adult-child relationship.

A Trust Building Program

The program is a series of concepts identified as *Steps*. The plan for each step includes background for understanding the concepts, working strategies for an adult to use, and activities for the child. The one-to-one work begins with *commitment*—the establishing of rapport and credibility. Other concepts include *confidentiality, limits,* and *dependency.* The use of facts and management of behavior are included in order to help children control what they say and do.

There are instructions on how to terminate these one-to-one sessions. Understandably, follow-up may require some continued support through additional meetings focused on specific steps where more help is needed. How to offer support in a crisis is explained and there are suggestions on how to communicate with parents.

Each step is illustrated by fictional, continuing stories which feature Shelly, age six, combined first and second grade; Roger, nine, a third-grader; Tim, eleven, a sixth-grade boy; and Mary, thirteen, a student in a middle school. You will see how each benefits from the one-to-one work on some of the problems they face and the progress they make through trusting in a caring adult.

> **Trust is the key to a child's attitude toward self and the world. Trust is the antecedent of all learning, of responsibility, and of self-discipline.**

The Meaning of Trust

Trust goes beyond reassurance. It is a bond, substantiated by honesty, consistency, dependability, and caring. Trust is a "bundle of attitudes" that denotes *unconditional acceptance.* It allows for good days and bad days. It permits kids to be kids. Children who trust feel protected and respected. They become willing to improve in many ways. . . . Trust must be built. It doesn't just happen. Adults engineer the program.

A Trust Building Program:

- provides enough consistent, positive acceptance to convince the Child Who Hurts that an adult can be trusted.

- helps a child become more self-accepting.

- helps a child acquire a positive attitude toward self, school, and others—to feel respected.

- helps a child manage what he or she says or does.

- helps a child internalize that he or she *can be special* to one adult.

- reminds a child that improvements *can be permanent*—can grow and grow—even if there are still problems at home.

- magnifies the importance of trustworthiness as a way of life—as basic to respect and communication in all relationships.

A Trust Building Program has limitations:

- It is *not* to change a child's personality.

- It is *not* to fix or repair problems at home.

- It is *not* to correct any difficulties the child may have with other adults.

The adaptation of the steps of a Trust Building Program in a regular classroom or other group setting is included. There are suggestions for follow-up in one-to-one sessions.

This program, as defined, is a *Child-Adult program*. It is child-focused, and does *not* expand to parent problem-solving. However, there is content on how to communicate with parents and how to respond should a problem with parents arise.

You are the key. Your relationship with the child is pivotal. A Trust Building Program is a challenge. It is not an overwhelming task. It can be enormously satisfying.

Ruth P. Arent

Things to Know
Before Starting the Program

CHILDREN WHO HURT VS.
CHILDREN WHO HATE

Realistically, there are some severely damaged children who are readily recognized as Children At Risk. These children require more professional help than a Trust Building Program provides. In this text, they are identified as Children Who Hate.

   The way to differentiate between Children Who Hurt and Children Who Hate can be seen through their various symptoms, (see Page 2). Section 8 suggests how to handle Children Who Hate. These children, with very few exceptions, have known defective attachments. A defect can only be repaired when there is trust. To help Children Who Hate may take years and years.

Children are entitled to love, respect, and trusting relationships. They didn't become Children Who Hurt or Children Who Hate on purpose. Someone threw rocks at their rainbows.

   The renowned child psychiatrists Drs. Fritz Redl and David Wineman introduced the concept of Children Who Hate in 1951. The subtitle to their book reads, *The Disorganization and Breakdown of Behavior Controls.* The symptoms of Children Who Hate cited in this text go beyond the Redl descriptions. This list is intended to expedite identification in order that the reader of this book may judge the severity of problems and use such information when selecting children with whom to work. Children Who Hurt can benefit greatly from a Trust Building Program. Children Who Hate need to be referred to a professional psychologist, psychiatrist, or other mental health specialist. Some need placement and/or medical attention.

Most schools provide special programs for the Child Who Hates, and community resources are available.

WHAT HAS HAPPENED TO CAUSE HURT?

Family Problems or Relationships Can Cause Hurt

Often Children Who Hurt have lost someone with whom they had a close bond. Stressful situations—divorce, death, fights—even suicide convey the message that life in the family is unsafe. Some family relationships are seriously infected with rejection, criticisms, violence, contradictions, and neglect. Children believe that no one cares about them. They learn that adults are *not to be trusted*—that adults sometimes make decisions or do things that hurt others. Squalid environments, poor nutrition, chronic stress, social maladjustments and parental addictions and self-esteem problems invariably hurt children in many ways. Children Who Hurt come from all walks of life.

> **All families know stress. Most relationships have their ups and downs. Some children cope well while others do not.**

Children in stressful family situations blame themselves. Self-blame is costly. *Self-blame destroys self-esteem.* Frequently, children shoulder the blame if a parent dies or leaves home. "My report card was bad. Mom and Dad had a fight about it. Dad left two weeks later. I'm sure that the fight about my report card caused the divorce. It's all my fault."

Feelings of helplessness destroy self-esteem, too. Children feel powerless: "I couldn't stop my daddy from drinking. He was drunk the night he got killed." Abused children feel guilty as well. Children Who Hurt *desperately* need to hear, "It was not your fault."

Children remain hurt when familes do not recover from difficult situations or are unable to repair strained, destructive relationships. Children cannot recover alone. They remain confused. They feel disrespected, incompetent, and fearful. Each is haunted by the questions *"What will happen to me? Will someone ever care for me?"* These questions *hurt*. The hurt persists in school, in a bubble bath, at birthday parties, and at Christmas.

School Experiences Can Cause Hurt

School experiences can squash a child's self-esteem. Competition can annihilate the losers—the ones with the fewest stars on the charts. Research tells us that children over the age of seven are particularly vulnerable to public scorn or humiliation. A mistake in a spelling bee may be traumatic for an insecure person.

Young children take the blame if there is a teacher-child mismatch. Kids in slow reading groups think that they are dumb. Immature, slow developers may annoy others, especially if the teacher scolds them a lot. They are not mature enough to understand that many teachers prefer well-behaved, motivated learners. The sensitive child will overreact if the teacher becomes impatient or hostile. The child will feel rejected. School becomes an unsafe place to be.

> It's hard to feel good about me if I think my teacher doesn't like me! If my teacher doesn't like me, I must be bad. Will I ever be okay?

Learning Difficulties Can Cause Hurt

I AM NO GOOD is a badge that a child may picture all day long. It destroys self-esteem, and it prevents children from trusting that any adult can help them to be successful—yet they know they must have help.

A child with learning problems may have serious misperceptions about school and teachers. These need to be confronted. For many reasons, special help is needed. The teacher must be aware of the child's strengths and weaknesses and deal with memory problems, distractability, hyperactivity, poor social skills and lack of self-acceptance. Grades, promotions, and placements are powerful messages that can affect a child's sense of personal worth. It takes a long time to overcome learning problems. A Trust Building Program includes strategies which encourage academic improvement or successes. These successes are orchestrated into the one-to-one work which focuses on self-esteem and improved behavior.

CARETAKERS NEED ENCOURAGEMENT

In order to maintain your enthusiasm for the intensive work demanded by the intricate aspects of the Trust Building sessions, *it is of utmost importance that you feel good about yourself.* The uncomplicated questionnaire to be completed (See Page 178) is reportedly most reassuring. Counselors, teachers, and psychologists welcome the opportunity to reaffirm their well-being. Mentors, youth leaders, nurses, and other caretakers are also grateful for encouragement and applause.

Given the burden of classroom responsibilities, it has been demonstrated that *teachers feel more comfortable when they do not carry more than two Trust Building Programs at one time*. Counselors, mentors, and others may have more time available and can schedule one-to-one sessions with more children.

Special Message to Teachers

Teaching has been described as a lonely profession. Many teachers settle into their separate classrooms, feeling isolated from others in the building. Many feel especially lonely when they want support in the management of disruptive kids or suggestions on how to fill the void for children whose lives are parched emotionally and need to be redirected toward success and happiness.

Counselors can offer such support. Materials that counselors provide can be quite useful, even if the person-to-person contact is limited. This book is intended as just such an offering. This book's **Activities Pages** can be passed back and forth—the concepts applicable to both office or classroom.

This does not represent a chain of command. Teachers and counselors must confer together regarding Children Who Hurt. Identifying children and developing ways to work with them can be a multidisciplinary enterprise. Counselors have opportunities to deal with families, help children in crises, confer with community helpers and special services. Teachers know the children intimately and can help set behavioral and academic goals. Each enriches the knowledge of the other. Together they can discuss the application of the concepts of the Trust Building Program for a particular boy or girl. They can encourage each other.

No one is a second-class citizen when it comes to helping these selected children; Trust Building Programs are not to be the private property of any one group of grownups.

1 BEFORE YOU BEGIN A TRUST BUILDING PROGRAM

HOW TO SELECT A CHILD FOR ONE-TO-ONE WORK

With this background, proceed into the Trust Building Program by first selecting the children with whom you will have the one-to-one meetings. Chances are you can already picture some children you know who could benefit from your help. Counselors, social workers and others have many referrals. Teachers readily identify children who are malfunctioning.

To support your impressions, it is necessary to evaluate the severity of the symptoms that you observe, identify a child's strength or wellness and consider possible outcomes from the work you will do together through use of a **Struggles Chart** (see Page 4).

Recognize the Severity of the Symptoms the Child Displays

Children Who Hurt are differentiated from Children Who Hate on Page 2. Although you may witness an array of symptoms, some of which may denote a deeprooted problem, refer to the following *three criteria*: How long have the symptoms persisted? How damaging is the problem? How frequently do the symptoms occur? These questions can help you decide if a child can be helped or is too damaged and requires *intensive* help. For example, Children Who Hurt may have an occasional temper tantrum. Children Who Hate exhibit a deeper anger in many ways *most of the time*. There is no set configuration of answers. Your judgment plus your list of symptoms should be sufficient.

Symptoms to Note

The following array of symptoms can help you select a child. Any one child will seldom display all of the symptoms listed.

Children Who Hurt:	*Children Who Hate:*
are occasionally spacy	lose touch with reality
occasionally tell lies, steal, destroy property	become habitual liars
	become kleptomaniacs
are moody, angry, and depressed but able to function	may be suicidal
make most decisions appropriately, may act out, may seek attention	may be profoundly depressed, require medicine, hospitalization
	isolate, display lack of bonding
learn in school though the pattern is inconsistent, below grade level	are habitual truants, have behavior problems, may be older than peers
have impaired ability to memorize and concentrate	are addicted to drugs, alcohol, sexual acting out
have poor peer relationships	are a danger to self or others
keep adults at a distance	do not know the difference between right and wrong—lack a conscience
may be withdrawn, isolated most of the time	become cynical, reject belief that human relationships can be compassionate
are immature	
manipulate	seek rejection as a way of life
have a poor self-concept	become cruel, callous—especially evident with small children and animals
have not been brutalized per se; have known some consistent attention	become the children nobody wants, have very few deep relationships
may have satisfactory relationship with peers or siblings	may be totally turned off to learning, except survival skills
learn—when they like the teacher	may have been brutalized, abandoned, or have experienced frequent rejections
	have consistent problems with authority

The child you select is under control most of the time and readily distinguishes right from wrong. The child may display symptoms when under stress in a particular situation and not in others.

Observe Indicators of Wellness, Strengths, or Appropriate Coping Behaviors. Your goal in working with children is to reinforce strengths and wellness, and provide the confidence needed for the child to let go of symptoms and learn new ways to cope, learn, and relate to others. The following list of Indicators of Wellness serves *two purposes*: It helps in the selection process because it provides clues that the child can be helped, and spells out specific observable behaviors that can show how a child has benefited from a Trust Building Program. It can be used as a checklist before, during, or after a Trust Building Program.

Indicators of Wellness Children May Display

They:

Tell the truth.

Accept compliments, perhaps affection.

Express appreciation, timely enthusiasm, and joy.

Display a positive attitude toward others—at least some of the time.

Feel optimistic that they can succeed in school.

Display empathy, sensitivity, perhaps tenderness.

Are able to memorize.

Feel empowered to express opinions, be assertive, stand up for themselves, and handle themselves without losing control.

Work hard to let go of anger in appropriate ways.

Enjoy their own company.

Display creativity.

Trust Your Feelings and Reactions.   Your intuition and common sense are important. *Select children about whom you feel hopeful or optimistic.* You will be able to appreciate certain qualtities about these children that will inspire you.

You may or may not know a child's history or be acquainted with past traumas. Such knowledge does not have to influence your selection. Your work focuses on the now. It will build on strengths, not weaknesses.

Children Who Hurt can display empathy. This is a sign of their wellness. The ability to empathize also distinguishes Children Who Hurt from more severely damaged children.

You Can Foresee Some Measures or Signs of Improvement Based on the Wellness You Have Noted. Indicators of improvement may include improvement in attendance, punctuality, misconduct reports, grades, attitude, or behavior. If you are a teacher, you will note improvements in responsiveness, peer acceptance, attitude, countenance, and perhaps academic performance. Some symptoms will diminish. Others will disappear.

Improvements reinforce the efforts of everyone involved. *Be aware that children, while learning to trust, will have setbacks.* No one is to blame for that. Regressive episodes are to be expected.

Take your time in selecting the children. Become familiar with the Steps of the Trust Building Program before you begin. **Strategies Pages** describe the concepts and provide instruction. Read over the Activities Pages.

For many of you, this program may simply help you structure your work more effectively, through the program's identified concepts and guidelines for application. You may already have an excellent rapport with a child and find that parts of this program enhance what you're doing or give it new direction.

THE USE OF STRUGGLES CHARTS

A *Struggles Chart* (see the sample in Figure 1 on Page 4) is a form on which to record observations of children's behaviors and the consequences that occurred. The forms are for brief notations—not for details or analysis. They help

Charlie					
Date	Behavior observed	How long?	Reaction of others	Results 1–2 weeks	Other observations
11/6	Nasty, sarcastic	All day, 3rd day this week	Indifferent, walked away, told to shut up	Beginning to withdraw	Dirty
11/12	Tired, depressed, very quiet	1st day	Ignored	Loss of interest in school	Withdrawn, sleepy
11/18	Tantrum followed by depression	3 times	Ridiculed, some name calling	Becoming isolated	Doesn't want to go home
11/19	Staring at others, afraid to approach	2 days	Ignored		Day-dreaming

Figure 1

the adult avoid becoming emotionally involved with the children's problems.

Struggles Charts are useful before and during the Trust Building Program. Initially, they are used by the adults to help select children who do not trust. Through the duration of the Trust Building Program, the adult should continue to use the Struggles Charts, and boys and girls who can write are invited to fill in a modified version as well. Observations will denote changes, improvements, and help delineate problems. When children note their own struggles, it promotes their involvement and awareness.

Children Who Hurt may accept notations on a written document more readily than if they are told. This is true for both positive and critical observations.

How to Use a Struggles Chart

Before the Program Begins Observe the child for a minimum of one week in school or three or four sessions in your office, at meetings such as youth groups, or Sunday School.

The First Four Columns Apply at This Time Column One (see Figure 1) is for time and/or date. This helps to clarify whether the problem is a one-time event or crisis, or should be considered habitual or chronic. Column Two, *Behavior Observed*, may include what the child did as well as attitude, verbalizations, etc. Column Three, *How Long or Frequency*, helps the observer to stay focused on the struggle or child. Column Four, *Reaction of Others*, is to substantiate your impression that this is a Child Who Hurts. Children want to be popular and to have friends. Observe reactions such as "Ignored" or "Ridiculed." These are powerful statements.

The Trust Building Program is not for rehashing the past. However, notations on a Struggles Chart can serve as guidelines for work to be done and goals to be set.

When You Invite a Child into a Trust Building Program Select some notations to discuss with the child to support your invitation. There is no need to comment on each notation. Emphasize that you are concerned that children who have these difficulties may be unhappy and that you want to be a supportive person.

During the Weeks of the Trust Building Program Filling in Column Five, *Results after 1 or 2 weeks (or more)*, gives a long term perspective to what is going on and the progress that is being made. Column Six, *Other Observations*, enriches your understanding of the child.

Positive statements are important, too. Express how pleased you are with changes and improvements. Consider saying, "I know it is a *struggle* to learn to stop saying mean things and to say nice things instead."

When children fill in a chart of their own, they are empowered to focus on reactions or results without having to hear anyone say, "I told you so," or "I warned you."

The positive notations provide a checklist of strengths and indicators of wellness. See Page 109 on **How to End a Trust Building Program** for suggestions on how to give children ongoing support and deal with weaknesses that still may exist. A Trust Building Program doesn't perform miracles. It is a method to diminish hurt and instill greater self-confidence. Invariably there will still be some symptoms of hurt, some inappropriate behaviors, or discouraging, angry attitudes. Refer to this list as you decide whether or not the child is strong enough to phase out of the Trust Building Program. You will delineate indicators of improved self-esteem. That is one major goal.

> **Educational consultant Jim Fay writes, "Children who do not learn how to struggle are not able to make the effort to succeed at school."* Children Who Hurt know many struggles at home, which have been damaging. With their Struggles Chart at school, they can note changes and mastery. Their improved sense of competency will help them with their struggles at home.**

THE ISSUE OF PARENT PERMISSION

Most parents understand that counselors meet with a child on a one-to-one basis routinely. This is *not* a standard procedure for many teachers.

Parent permission for a child to meet alone with a teacher has become a controversial matter. Some districts require permission for anything—save formal class contacts. For a myriad of reasons, these districts are reluctant to permit teachers to take time with individual children for much-needed special encouragement. Other districts have a more liberal policy. It is essential for you to know what policies apply in your school district. This applies to teachers, counselors, nurses, social workers and others.

If parental permission is necessary, you can write a form requesting permission for the child to meet for "special encouragement" or to "enhance self-esteem" or to "motivate the child to improve academic work." You want children to *learn to trust that someone in school is earnestly concerned about their progress.* If you introduce the word "trust" in this manner, it will harmonize with the title of this book—you will truly create a Trust Building Program.

Talk to a child about the possibility of the one-to-one sessions—for

---

* Jim Fay. *Success With the Reluctant Learner,* 2207 Jackson St., Golden, CO 80401: School Consultant Services, Inc. 1985.

encouragement—and explain *immediately* that parent permission is necessary. Make it a brief, positive, factual statement. This clarifies your position.

Some parent refusals may be expected because some parents do not want their children in an unfamiliar program for a variety of reasons.

If permissions are not necessary and the children tell their parents, that is their privilege. This does not alter your position. You affirm with each child that *you will not share what goes on in one-to-one sessions except, as bound legally, to report neglect and abuse.* **What you talk about is between the two of you.**

For suggestions on how to communicate with parents once a program is underway, see pages 163–169, **Messages to Parents: A Special Art, A Necessary Task.**

Reminders for Adults   Reaffirm your commitment that success is your way of life. Be determined that you will succeed in helping Children Who Hurt find their strengths and build on them. Call these strengths *signs of wellness.* Help these children begin to expand their wellness and become strong enough not to feel overwhelmed, exploited, or victimized by others.

HOW TO CONDUCT ONE-TO-ONE SESSIONS: A RECOMMENDED PATTERN TO FOLLOW

A one-to-one session is not a casual get-together. It is a short meeting—an uninterrupted time for you to discuss what you consider important and for the children to share what they *want* to share. In addition, there are documents to look over such as the Struggles Charts and Activities Pages. You will see each other a minimum of *twice a week* for *seven to ten weeks*, that approximates *fourteen to twenty meetings* in which to present all the steps of the program and to delve into problems.

> **Flexibility is the key. Each session will be different.**

Although each session you conduct will be different, *a basic pattern is essential.* The pattern will begin to feel familiar to the child. The consistency and structure will enhance the Trust Building Program.

Open With a Warm Greeting

"I'm glad to see you today."

"I've been looking forward to our meeting."

"I've been thinking about you a lot since we talked together on Tuesday."

Give Feedback

Refer to something discussed in the last one-to-one session.

"I'm glad you told me about how mean your sister is to you. Now I understand why you are so sensitive when other kids put you down. We'll have to work on that."

Refer to Something Positive That You Have Observed

Note: Use compliments sparingly. Children Who Hurt often mistrust verbal compliments. They may regard them as manipulations or an indication that you are not sincere.

"I noticed you haven't been critical of me for three days."

"I was glad to see you having fun with your friends in the cafeteria."

"You did a good job on that book report."

Select a Concept from the Trust Building Program for Each One-to-One Session

Strategies Pages contain explanations and directions.

Each concept needs to be integrated into your relationship and communication. In other words, there should be ongoing reminders of early concepts such as confidentiality and limits. This is important. The child may forget or be unable to synthesize one concept with another.

Use the Word "Trust"

"I'm glad that you trust me enough to tell me about the problems in your art class."

"I like the fact that you come to me for help when you are upset. I feel that you are beginning to depend on me. That's part of trusting."

"I may not always be able to give you advice when you ask, but you can trust me when I say, 'I want you to be happy. You are special to me.'"

Start Your Self-Disclosure

Trust depends on mutual respect and sharing. The adult in a Trust Building Program is advised not to be too impersonal or formal but rather to be authentic and spontaneous. Openness helps to break down certain barriers which keep frightened children from learning to trust. Many parents, for a number of reasons, are not open with their children. *You may be the first person who takes time to share or openly talks about sensitive thoughts.*

Self-disclosure can be quite superficial yet successfully reinforce the bond that you are working to achieve. Consider telling about your family life as a child, your interests, food preferences, or books, movies, or TV shows that you enjoy.

On another level, you may discuss your friendships, family ties, or concerns about matters such as peace, the environment, pollution, and so forth.

It is not necessary or advisable to talk about money matters, your sexuality, health concerns that could create worry, or your opinion of other people—save some public figures, perhaps.

Above all, make "I" statements that relate to your relationship with the Child Who Hurts:

"I'm glad I'm getting to know you better."

"I didn't realize we were both interested in animals."

"I often think of you when I see a lovely sunset."

Do not anticipate that such comments will instigate discussion. They are important as reinforcements of the relationship. You *model* trust. You are open and honest. Stories may be welcome with lead-in lines like

"Yesterday, I had to get new tires for my car."

"My little boy learned to ride a bike."

"I watched an interesting show on TV about spiders."

"When I was a kid, I. . . ."

From the child's point of view, your honesty about yourself may be the most important part of a Trust Building Program. In dysfunctional families, there is seldom honest self-disclosure—if there is any at all.

> The process of learning to trust is not steady. The pace will be determined by how readily a child is able to believe that you are for real.

Use Activities Pages

The Activities Pages amplify definitions and provide a combination of activities for application and reinforcement. Activities Pages are found at the end of almost every step. They provide ideas for open discussion.

Use Struggles Charts

Adult and child can look over notations on Struggles Charts and select items for acclaim, explanation, or problem solving.

Open Discussion—10 to 15 Minutes

Content builds from whatever you or the child choose. If it is a continuation of whatever was discussed at the last session, it may be necessary to postpone the introduction of new steps or concepts until the next appointment.

Remain Child-Focused

When a child tells you something disturbing about a parent or another teacher, focus on the child and how he or she feels and copes. You may want to exclaim, "What a mean thing for a dad to say to his kid," but *that is not okay*. Be careful—*do not criticize a parent*. The child may need to ventilate to you but *family loyalty* is fundamental. Revelations about bad experiences, episodes, nasty words or problems that take place among the members of the family are *not* to be interpreted as a lack of loyalty.

> If you imply or say anything critical about a parent, you may undermine or cut off the child's trust in you.

Consider Play-Doh® for Young Children

In the 10- to 15-minute open discussion times, some children will talk more freely if their hands are occupied. You may want to let them handle Play-Doh®, clay, crayons, or colored pipe cleaners while they talk. It is not necessary to comment about what they do with them.

Ending the Session

Make a positive remark about what you have discussed—"I'm proud of what you are doing. I know you will try hard not to lose your temper."
Reaffirm your appointment for the next session.

Use Affirmations

Each session will end with an affirmation. Introduce affirmations in the first session. An *affirmation* is a positive thought that is selected to be repeated out loud and/or written repeatedly. It should be repeated every day for at least two weeks. (See **Use of Affirmations**, Page 11).

THE USE OF AFFIRMATIONS

Affirmations are positive statements that people repeat in order to acknowledge that they are worthy. This builds self-esteem. More than one affirmation can be used at a time. Some are sensitive, and some superficial.

Teach Children Who Hurt how to use affirmations. Allow time for them at the close of each one-to-one session. These are tools to help get rid of old negative attitudes. They support improvements and help build self-esteem. They help "open up" a child's willingness to experience trust. Adults are urged to use affirmations, too.

Sample Affirmations for Children:

I deserve to have someone listen to me.

I deserve to be recognized when I do something for someone else.

I deserve help when I am trying hard in school.

I deserve to be taken care of.

I deserve friends.

I deserve to make mistakes.

I deserve love, affection, and understanding.

Sample Affirmations for Adults:

I deserve to indulge myself—such as buying out-of-season fresh strawberries.

I deserve to express my feelings and thoughts.

I deserve the chance to enrich my life.

I deserve not to be a victim.

I deserve love, affection, and understanding.

An affirmation is a personal statement that may be shared with another but is not open to discussion. You may want to note yours in a journal.

MEET FOUR CHILDREN WHO HURT AND FOUR GROWNUPS WHO CARE

FICTIONAL STORIES BASED ON CASE HISTORIES

Shelly, Roger, Tim, and Mary struggle as they learn to trust. Their stories are interesting. You will become devoted to each of these kids. They are lovable.

These fictional stories, based on case histories, describe how the *steps* or *concepts* of the Trust Building Program are handled by the adult in one-to-one sessions.

Shelly is six, in the first/second grade combination class; Roger, nine, is in the third grade; Tim, eleven, is a sixth-grade boy; and Mary, thirteen, is in Middle School. The younger children meet with teachers; Mary and her counselor work together.

MEET SHELLY AND MISS TIPTON, A FIRST-YEAR TEACHER

Shelly is six years old and in a first and second grade combination class. She lives with her father and her grandmother. Her mother and father divorced when she was seven months old. She sees her mother occasionally and receives cards and presents for her birthday. When she was living alone with her father, she had a series of female baby sitters—some of whom were not very attentive or affectionate. She appears to be suspicious of all women—excepting her grandmother.

Shelly resembles a cat who is ready to scratch—defensive, unpleasant and surly. She has an unusually large vocabulary for one who appears so unstable. Her attention span is unpredictable. She likes books, film strips, and computers. In group situations, she is an exhibitionist and a jitterbug. She seems to have no respect for others' rights. Other children don't like her. She has never been invited to a birthday party. When her grandmother picks her up at school, Shelly is soft and sweet. This has been observed by her teacher.

Miss Tipton is a first-year teacher. Her goal in working with Shelly is to increase her softness, decrease her defensiveness, help her feel successful as a learner, and work on her social skills.

Unlike the others in her class, Shelly rarely talks about herself. She talks about her dolls, the library books that her grandmother gets for her, her favorite TV shows, and a cousin who comes to visit. If someone asks her about her mom directly, she squints her eyes, which gives the appearance of anger and held-back tears. She seldom smiles. She is private, unsettled, and uncomfortable physically.

When Miss Tipton asks Shelly to do anything creative, like painting or crafts, Shelly destroys what she does. It is as if permanency or attachment is more than she can handle. Her favorite expression is "I hate that" whether talking about food, the lunch room, the clothes she is wearing, or the music the teacher is playing.

Her bonds to her father and grandmother provide her with enough security that she would not be considered a Child Who Hates. Miss Tipton is convinced that Shelly could respond to another woman in addition to her grandmother. This would help her develop self-acceptance and healthy behavior. Once Shelly can learn to manage her anger, her classmates should become more friendly. Her teacher undertands that the child may harbor sadness because of her mother, but her classmates know nothing about Shelly's history. They just don't like to be around her. Shelly's habits must change. This will take time. It will be one benefit of a Trust Building Program.

Miss Tipton is a quiet, gentle women. She encourages all the children as she comments about how quickly they get ready to listen to a story or how polite they are to each other. She does not raise her voice but remains motionless and silent in order to get their attention. Other members of the faculty see her as shy and sweet. She has a fine understanding of kids—really loves the young girls and boys.

MEET ROGER AND MRS. SNYDER, AN EXPERIENCED TEACHER

Roger is a third grader, nine and a half years old. He doesn't like himself. He has learned to ignore his teacher when she praises him or says "Roger, I'm so proud of you." He has heard nice comments before. He hears the nice things that she says to the other children, too. That's what teachers do, he thinks. He is convinced that Mrs. Snyder doesn't like him any more than other grownups like him. They all criticize him a lot and seem bossy. When a grownup is friendly, Roger is certain that it is a trick to get him to settle down, finish his work, or take out the trash. It's not because they like me, he believes. Roger wishes he were "special" to someone. He would be happy if some adult really enjoyed spending time with him. But no one gives him a hug—much less a kiss goodnight.

Roger knows that he is not dumb. He doesn't have to go to remedial reading or the resource room for help. However, he's never been in the top reading group. Roger figures that when grownups don't like you, you don't get to be in the top reading group. He can pass tests. Sometimes his paper is posted on the bulletin board but he pretends not to notice. He has no special friends. No one asked about the big scratch on his arm. He doesn't feel important to anyone. He wishes he didn't have to come to school.

From outside appearances, Roger comes from an average home. There are three siblings; Roger is the middle child. He gets along in his own way. He is hypnotized by TV from 4 p.m. until bedtime on school days and all weekend as well. His mother never asks him what he's watching. Dad never comments either. Occasionally Roger joins them for dinner. Most of the time he eats alone. He is sure that no one cares if he is there or not, and besides, his brother and sister interrupt when he has something to say. He remembers that Mom spanked him when he broke a window and once when he screamed at his sister. Roger feels like a piece of furniture at his house.

Occasionally home is a scary place to be. When Dad has had too much to drink, he and Mom scream at each other. Roger has seen his Dad hit his mother—hit her hard. He covers his eyes or runs out of the house when Dad loses his temper. Roger has been beaten, too. He can't figure out why things are fine for a while and then build up to another big blow. After Mom gets hit, all is calm again. He's never sure when Dad will lose control again. He worries about his mom when he is in school. Suppose Mom gets hit and has to go to the hospital—or dies? He wishes he could talk to his mom about this, but he wouldn't dare.

When Mr. and Mrs. Conrad are called about Roger's school problems, they threaten to take away the TV, but this never happens. Sometimes they tease him. They'll call, "Hey, Problem Child, it's time to get dressed."

Once in a while the phone rings for Roger. One of his classmates wants to come over and play or borrow a bike. Once he was invited to a birthday party, but his mom didn't show up to take him.

Roger loved preschool. There were trikes and swings and lots of things to do. Later, in kindergarten, he felt unimportant, unnoticed—just the seventh space down on the Star Chart. At Show and Tell, he told about TV—never about his family or even his dog. When his dog died, he figured no one would care. Dad said something about getting a new one, but he never did.

Roger hurts inside. He is a fragile, frightened child. The ongoing disinterest of his parents makes him feel worthless and angry. School is not important to him. He needs help. He is not mentally ill.

Mrs. Snyder is an experienced teacher who wants to enrich the lives of each of her students. She reads them classic poems by Robert Louis Stevenson or Lewis Carroll. The field trips she plans are to interesting art shows and musical events. There are times when Roger's passive or negative attitude bothers Mrs. Snyder. It is in marked contrast to the enthusiasm of the other boys and girls.

MEET TIM AND MR. ATKINS, THE GYM TEACHER

Tim attends middle school. He feels like a misfit and is becoming afraid of school. He feels inadequate. He is unduly sensitive to criticisms, suggestions, and poor grades. After each report card, he gets seriously depressed. His teachers have been encouraging to him, but he has given up on himself and is convinced that no one really cares if he does well.

Tim started school at five years and three months. Some of his classmates were almost seven years old. Tim wanted to play, explore, and tease. The others were ready to settle down and learn to read and write. His teacher was nice, and she kept telling him he could do better if he would only try. Tim became confused. His report card said that he was immature. He understood that to mean that he was no good and that whatever he did should have been done in another way. He has never had a chance to feel confident.

Tim's father was killed when Tim was three. Tim remembers that his mother cried a lot and that they had to move into his grandmother's home. No one has ever told him what happened to his dad. He is confused about this, too—wondering if maybe he did something to cause the accident. His mother has had several boyfriends. None of them has ever made Tim feel special even though they would take him to the movies or a baseball game. His mother is seldom home. She works hard and always has a boyfriend around when she is home. Tim and his mother don't have much to say to each other. Tim has two best friends. When he is depressed, he gets "snappy" and will say something sarcastic. He doesn't mean to be nasty but he is perceived that way. Tim is an only child. Sometimes he wishes he had a brother or sister he could talk to.

It wasn't until the end of second grade that someone discovered Tim's visual problem. What was mistaken for "sloppy work" or "no effort" was evidence that he was unable to copy off the board accurately or line up his numbers properly. He had acquired the habit of asking teachers to repeat directions for him. When he believed that his teacher got annoyed at this, he stopped asking. He then made no effort to do his work and blamed his teacher.

His eyes still give him problems. He reverses letters, cannot visualize how to spell words, and cannot "carry over" from one math column to the next. His handwriting is illegible because he labors with a white-knuckle approach to each task. His written work is usually incomplete and he wants permission to use a computer but this cannot be arranged.

Tim is confused about his strengths and weaknesses. Because of his learning problems, he is even more confused about why some things make sense and others don't. He uses the resource room and works with an aide. He told his mother that his teachers don't treat him like he's stupid and they don't put him down. Tim puts himself down.

Occasionally, Tim thinks about dropping out of school as soon as he can, but some of the kids are fun, and besides, he is too young to get a job. And he likes gym. Mr. Atkins lets him help with the equipment. Mr. Atkins enourages him to be a good runner. Sometimes he pats him on the back. This is the only affection Tim gets.

Unless Tim has a caring commitment from an adult—preferably a man—he may give up on learning. He may become even more confused and more seriously depressed. He can find ways to be successful. Perhaps he may even express his feelings about being a fatherless boy.

Mr. Atkins is a large man whose ready smile endears him to students. He teaches gym but does not prearrange the children into permanent teams in order to minimize competition. All teams are a mixture of good and not-so-good athletes. He stresses cooperation, enjoying each other, and good sportsmanship. He wants the children to improve their own performances—to acquire greater endurance, for example.

Mr. Atkins is somewhat aloof with the other members of the faculty. He is one of five males on the staff—the only Black person. He frequently talks with others about the local football team or some school policy, but he doesn't discuss himself. He cares deeply about the students—has great empathy for lonely boys. Tim is one of those lonely boys.

MEET MARY AND MRS. BRYCE, THE COUNSELOR

Mary is a very pretty eighth-grade girl, thirteen years old. She has piercing dark eyes, lovely long hair, and a peach complexion. She is aware of how attractive she is.

She behaves in a way that is manipulative and crusty. She's quite capable of learning. She doesn't pay attention or make any effort to participate in class. She concentrates just enough to get along but seldom produces any work. In written work, she shows a flicker of humor.

Mary enjoys being a leader of a group of girls who appear to worship her. She says that's why she comes to school. "It makes me feel okay when I watch them fight over who gets to sit next to me."

In the counselor's office, Mary is stoic. She was caught smoking in the girls' room for the third time. She doesn't intend to stop smoking and is curious to see what Mrs. Bryce has to say about that.

Mary is the youngest of six children in a family of independent individuals. Her brothers and sisters used to play with her when she was little, but now they are all out on their own. Her mother is a bitter woman who occasionally shares her "soft side," as Mary describes it. Mary's mother has had a bad heart for the past six years and can no longer work. She spends her time on the phone or watching TV. Being dependent on her husband makes her angry. The husband may or may not come home for two or three days at a time. Mary's father is critical and sarcastic when he is there. One of Mary's brothers told her that she was an unwanted child. Mary believes this.

Mary is becoming streetwise. Her flirtatious behavior borders on seductiveness. Mrs. Bryce is determined to develop a trust relationship with her in order to help her focus on school and use her apt intelligence. She feels certain that Mary can use her potential to become the competent pediatric nurse that she would like to be. Unless Mary becomes convinced that her success is important to at least one adult, she may begin a series of self-destructive, antisocial behaviors that are difficult to stop.

Mrs. Bryce has decided to refer to the Trust Building Program as a Confidence Building Program because she knows that Mary would scoff at the word "trust."

Mrs. Bryce is the envy of the entire faculty. She is slim and tall and models a collection of bright, classy clothes. She has a unique assortment of scarves—displayed creatively. Everyone likes Mrs. Bryce. She has been in the building for four years. The faculty trusts her judgment and recommendations. Others admire how she arranges time to see students who need help. Mary is one of those students.

Miss Tipton, Mrs. Snyder, Mr. Atkins and Mrs. Bryce will not delve into deeprooted problems or parental dilemmas. They will work intently to become *significantly important to the selected Child Who Hurts*. Each will handle the Trust Building Program concepts in his or her own style, and in time, each will become convinced that all efforts were worthwhile.

In the stories of Shelly, Roger, Tim, and Mary, you will see how each displays symptoms of hurt—how they venture into relationships, back off a bit, act out—but all end up with a sense of trust, feeling reasonably secure with the adult.

The sessions deal with feelings and problems, concepts and activities. For the most part, Miss Tipton, Mrs. Snyder, Mr. Atkins, and Mrs. Bryce follow the recommended pattern for one-to-one sessions. They make modifications as you probably will, too.

Each adult understood there was an appropriate, necessary time to let the boy or girl adapt a let's-keep-in-touch assurance. The students did not feel rejected. The end of the one-to-one sessions denoted a vote of confidence. However, everyone concerned did feel some regret.

> **On a branch that swings**
> **Sits a bird that sings**
> **Knowing that he has wings . . . .**

The adults helped the children to use their wings.

2 INVITE THE CHILD INTO A TRUST BUILDING PROGRAM

You have to be convincing, sensitive, and dedicated when you invite a child to take part in a Trust Building Program.*

Children Who Hurt may dream about having someone care about them, but they do not expect it ever to happen. An invitation to be alone with a counselor or teacher simply because they care, and not for a scolding or help with school work, is beyond their imagination.

Your invitation will cover a number of important statements. Expressed in your own way, consider these ideas:

I want to invite you into a program where you and I meet privately for a few minutes twice a week for a few weeks. I am concerned that you seem upset at times (or substitute another applicable reason gleaned from a Struggles Chart). I know that many kids don't like grownups much and don't trust them. They believe that no grownup really likes them. I don't know you well enough to know if that's how it is with you, but I worry when I see you upset. I want you to get to know me, and I would like to get to know you.

I call this a Trust Building Program because I want you to learn to trust me. There are a lot of ways I can prove that I can be trusted and that I care about you. I will try to help you feel good about yourself and this will help you understand that you are important to me. I want to encourage you to do your best in whatever you do.

It is important for you to know me. I will share things about myself from time to time. When both people in a relationship share openly, trust can develop.

* When parental permission is necessary, this invitation must not preempt parental approval. The fact that you mentioned the program and discussed parental permission must not be confused with your invitation to take part in a program.

There will be no homework. There will be no tests. There are interesting Activities Pages for you to do. Together we can decide how to use them.

I have a plan in mind that I'd like to begin with; we can change it if necessary. (Tell the child where you will meet, the time you will meet and the length of your proposed session.) "Our first meeting will be. . . . I'm looking forward to seeing you."

Note:

The initial invitation can be brief.

Reiterate your eagerness to begin the program.

There are no Activities Pages until sessions begin. Activities Pages are found at the end of each Step.

Affirmations are introduced later. (See Page 11.)

MISS TIPTON INVITES SHELLY INTO A TRUST BUILDING PROGRAM

Six-year-old Shelly grabs the red marker from Pam. She doesn't use it. It seems as if she wants to hold it so others at the table will get mad. She is controlling all five children. Each asks for the marker. Shelly says, "It's my turn. You wait," and still she doesn't take off the cap. When one of the girls complains to the teacher, Miss Tipton, Shelly watches. It doesn't seem to affect her one way or the other. Miss Tipton asks Shelly to share. Shelly says that she will when she is ready. She continues to hold the red marker.

Later Miss Tipton takes Shelly aside. "Shelly, I notice when a boy or girl seems unhappy or afraid. I write it down on something I call a Struggles Chart. I want to show you what I wrote about you because I want to begin a special program with you so you can talk about being unhappy or afraid."

"I am *not* unhappy or afraid either," Shelly snaps, "and my report card says that I am a good first-grade reader and that I use a lot of words that other kids don't use. My Grandma says I'm smart."

"I'm proud of what you have learned, but I am worried that you don't have friends. You are a smart girl, Shelly."

She put the Struggles Chart on the table. They read some of her notes. *Not friendly; Said "I don't like you" to Janie; Stood all by herself on the playground. Did not smile today.*

Miss Tipton repeats, "These notes tell me that we need time to talk together. I will see you in private twice a week for a few minutes. I'm sure that you will start to look forward to our talks soon. No one will know what we talk about."

Shelly doesn't say anything. She gets up from her chair, twirls around four or five times and says "What do you think of that twirl?" It is as if she hadn't heard what Miss Tipton has said. "You twirl well" Miss Tipton says, and then she repeats the invitation word for word. The little girl is quiet. "Shelly, I have seen how sweet you are with your grandmother, and I hope that some day you will feel comfortable with me. I want to help you but I can't do it without your help."

Shelly starts to bite her fingers. Without any enthusiasm, she says, "I'll talk to you if I have to, but don't ask me to draw pictures." Then she bristles, "I talk to my grandmother because I want to. If all this is because you want me to let the other kids have the markers, I can do that. You say I'm not friendly but they aren't friendly to me either."

"I'll arrange to see you tomorrow, Shelly," Miss Tipton says quietly. She recognizes that it will take a while before Shelly can accept closeness from any female other than her grandmother.

MRS. SNYDER INVITES ROGER INTO A TRUST-BUILDING PROGRAM

"I'm worried about how things are going this year, Roger. I want this to be the year when things turn around—when *you know* that you can do well in third grade and that you are special to me." Roger is not prepared to believe her. He has never believed that a teacher wants him to do well. He had always thought that when teachers said nice things, they said them to everybody. This sounds different. He decides to listen. He wonders what is coming next.

Mrs. Snyder explains about the Trust Building Program. "It's a plan for you and me to talk together—alone. It has to do with our relationship. It's a chance for you to get to know a grownup as a friend."

Roger doesn't say anything. In character, he puts his hands in his pockets and presses his fingers together. He feels confused, almost trapped. Mrs. Snyder is being too nice, he thinks. "What do I have to talk about?" he wants to know.

"Nothing special. Just what's on your mind." Roger stares at her. She continues, "I want you to get to know me—as a person, not as 'teacher.' I promise to be straight with you. I hope you will learn to trust me."

Roger shrugs his shoulders. He is glad that she didn't say anything about his mom and dad. Roger feels protective of them. She didn't put him down about his work. She didn't remind him of when he was sent to the office for hitting Matt.

He speaks quietly. "I'll see you a couple of times."

"I'm glad you said that, Roger. I'll look forward to our time together and I hope that you will, too. Let's start meeting for fifteen minutes after school on Wednesdays and Fridays. I can understand that it may feel weird to be asked to be in a special program with a teacher but *you're special.*"

Roger drops his eyes and walks off.

CHAPTER 2

MR. ATKINS INVITES TIM INTO A TRUST BUILDING PROGRAM

Mr. Atkins is a "natural" teacher and a father figure to many of the kids. He's quite concerned about Tim. Although he is aware that Tim has learning problems, Mr. Atkins sees him as depressed and in need of a friend.

When he approaches him in order to initiate a Trust Building Program, Tim doesn't pull away. To have Mr. Atkins ask him to stay a few minutes so that they can talk makes Tim feel pretty good. At first he wonders if he had done something wrong but is immediately assured that this is not so.

"You know, Tim, for a nice kid you sure know how to make others feel bad. I've noticed that you're alone a lot. And sometimes you look sad. My dad was killed when I was a little boy, and I know that your dad was killed, too. I want you to join me in a plan where we can talk about that and figure out some ways for you to be more friendly to other kids. How about meeting with me fifteen minutes before school on Tuesdays and Thursdays—right here in my office? Private talks, you know—nothing that anyone else has to know about—one-to-one like in basketball, but we'd be on the same team. How would you like that?"

Tim moves his eyes in Mr. Atkins direction, but doesn't say anything. Mr. Atkins continues, "Guess I'm the first teacher who has ever talked to you like this, Tim. Maybe it's because there is something about you I really like. I have a lot of faith in you. I want you to trust me. Besides, you take good care of this gym equipment." Tim smiles as he starts to walk toward the door.

"Do I have to ask my mom?"

"No, Tim, it's an in-school activity and it won't interfere with your classes. Later on, if you want me to, I can send some notes home with you about good work you do or some improvements. We can talk about it in a couple of weeks."

"Okay," Tim answers. "See you tomorrow."

MRS. BRYCE INVITES MARY INTO A TRUST BUILDING PROGRAM

"I am uncomfortable that it is under these circumstances that I am going to invite you into a Confidence Building Program. I don't want you to confuse our discussion about the no-smoking rules with this invitation."

She goes on to explain about the Confidence Building Program, emphasizing confidentiality, a regular meeting time and her strong convictions that Mary could be a much happier person—not a word about grades or attendance.

Mary is noncommital. "My life is okay. I don't need any counselor to tell me what's right and what's wrong with it." She stops abruptly. "But I want you to know that I think it was nice that you offered to see me again." She walks towards the door.

Mrs. Bryce repeats quietly "I have no mysterious list of things we should talk about. You can be the leader. Think it over if you will. I'll ask you again in a few days. It would be important to me." She appeals to Mary's need to be in a power position and does not budge from her own decision to reach out.

Mrs. Bryce and Mary pass in the hall. Mrs. Bryce smiles, and Mary, who is surrounded by friends, pretends that she doesn't see her. Several days later, Mrs. Bryce finds a benign excuse to call Mary to the office. She ends the brief encounter with a second invitation to join with her in the Confidence Building Program. "I can't do it alone," she says.

"How would I tell my friends?" Mary wants to know.

"That's up to you, Mary. Many kids drop by my office to talk. I hope you'll decide to come. I want to get to know you better."

After this invitation, Mary decides that Mrs. Bryce is sincere. Mary is just curious enough to want to check out what this program is all about.

3 THE PROGRAM

STEP ONE
COMMITMENT, CARING, AND CONFIDENTIALITY

Background

You may ask yourself an assortment of questions as you begin a Trust Building Program. You will think a lot about the goals you set and the procedures to follow. Misgivings will probably be replaced by a sense of anticipation and enthusiasm once the first session is underway. The boy or girl may or may not be responsive, but you can express your confidence that this Child Who Hurts can change—can feel better—*can learn to trust*. That's important reassurance for both of you.

You are prepared. You have read the recommended pattern to follow for each session. The first time you meet, describe the pattern that will be followed in each session and introduce the documents to the child. The idea of a pattern is appealing to children who are habitually disorganized. A pattern is an indication that you have done some planning on the child's behalf. This is a positive message, too.

The essential work of the first session builds around your positive attitude. It is a time to share and ask questions.

When you share brief anecdotes or details about yourself, remember this may be *a first* for the child who is listening. Many Children Who Hurt live with harried, depressed, or emotionally restricted adults who do not talk about themselves openly. Your sharing sets the stage for the open discussions in the sessions ahead.

When you repeat the goals of the program, which you may have already mentioned in your invitation, ask the child what ideas or questions he or she has about a Trust Building Program. The child may have nothing to say or not feel secure enough, as yet, to answer your questions. Children Who Hurt will withhold information because they wish to, because they may not remember, or perhaps haven't given any thought to their problems or situation.

> **The first session is an important event. Accept that the child will feel uncertain and may be curious and a little bit excited.**

Regarding Confidentiality   It is important to talk about confidentiality and prepare for possible exceptions. "What you share with me will be safe in this Trust Building Program" is a basic concept. Explain that there may be exceptions. "If you tell me something that has to do with abuse, your health or another serious problem, I may need to tell someone who can help. I have no choice when it comes to child abuse. By law, I must report it.

"If I do have to tell something to somebody else, I will tell you first. It does not mean that we will stop our one-to-one meetings." Most children do not respond to this explanation, but you have been open and honest, and protected both yourself and the program.

> **Confidentiality is one key to a child's willingness to trust.**

You may want to explain the rules that apply to one-to-one sessions. The brief list includes:

- No one is allowed to hurt oneself or anyone else.

- The adult will not share anything about the child without the child's knowledge and/or permission.

- (For older students) There will be no one-to-one sessions for anyone under the influence of drugs or alcohol.

The first session may be uncomfortable. There may be silences. There may be some giggling or complaining and many irrelevant questions. After a few sessions, the children will feel more secure. By then, you have shared about yourself and have not rehashed embarrassing or uncomfortable events from the past. Children do not always need "deep understanding" or insights in order to change. The positive rapport alone will motivate the children to come to their next appointments.

Reminders for Adults   Working with Children Who Hurt is the ultimate test of your professionalism. In the initial one-to-one session, you may feel "punctured" by a child's defensive sarcasm or rudeness. Nevertheless, you know the child cannot learn to trust alone. You decide to be the leader in this relationship; you anticipate that the work will be both frustrating and rewarding.

Strategies for One-to-One Sessions

Purpose: To express teacher enthusiasm and optimism that special meetings with the child will be helpful. To describe and follow the pattern for all one-to-one sessions. To introduce and offer the Struggles Chart. To introduce Activities Pages. To reiterate teacher or counselor commitment. To begin some self-disclosure. "I want you to learn to trust that you are special to me." To answer new questions the child may have about a Trust Building Program.

Directions: Express these ideas in your own style. Use your own vocabulary.

Important Statements the Child Should Hear "A Trust Building Program encourages you to ask what you want to know and to express what you want to express. You can ask about anything. I'm sure I won't know all the answers, but I'll do the best I can.

"I want you to feel free to explain whatever you need or want to explain.

"I will help you learn to choose what you say and do—so that you will not say or do things that you'll regret.

"We will discuss your attitude about many things. If you are discouraged or negative, we will try to work toward a brighter outlook.

"A Trust Building Program is not for your parents. It is to help you understand your reactions to things that happen and ways you can change, if necessary.

"In our work together, I will try to help you improve in school, manage your behavior, reaffirm your strengths, and hopefully, help you to become happy. I want you to succeed in whatever you do."

Introduce The Struggles Chart Show the student the chart you filled in prior to the invitation to the sessions. (See sample on Page 4.) Point out that you observed signs of sadness, fear, and/or anger. Be prepared to hear the child say, "You wrote that I looked unhappy. I am not unhappy—I'm mad. I'm mad because my mom divorced my dad." You may respond, "I write down what I see and hear. We will talk about your feelings."

Depending on reading ability, give the child a blank Struggles Chart to fill in between sessions. It is not an assignment. It is not mandatory. Suggest that the child bring the chart to each session for discussion. Tell the child that you will continue to fill in Struggles Charts. *Both of you* will keep track of good things and problems and compare to see where you agree and disagree. In the weeks ahead, the accumulation of good notations will be a record of the progress that the child has made. Negative notations designate areas that still need work.

Introduce Activities Pages Read over the directions in Activity 1–1 and select questions or activities. Give the child a copy. Emphasize that there are no right or wrong answers. Young children (nonreaders) can respond to the items as you read them aloud in each session.

Be aware that there are too many items on the Activities Pages to complete in one session, and that the discussions that follow must invariably be abbreviated. Use the Activities Pages items for as many sessions as necessary and combine them as you choose. Let the child decide whether he or she wants to keep them him- or herself or leave them in a file with the teacher.

Promote Discussion Encourage the child to express feelings, ask questions or mention any changes he or she would like to make.

A Trust Building Program should not rehash the past.

End of the Session

Negotiate times for regular sessions.

Set the time for the next one-to-one session.

End with an optimistic, personal statement: "I'm looking forward to seeing you. I'm sure we can. . . ."

Introduce affirmations. "I want to encourage you to get in the habit of saying something positive (nice) about yourself, such as 'I deserve friends.' Say it often. Say it as if you really believe it! This is called an affirmation. We will use them every time we meet."

Consider keeping a diary record of the one-to-one conversations. Note changes, facts shared, questions you may want to ask, or statements to be reiterated. Ask the child if he or she minds if you take notes during the sessions. Tell the child you are writing things down because it's important for you to remember. Share what you write down. Openness is essential to a Trust Building/Confidence Building Program. (Note-taking can make a child wonder about confidentiality. What if someone sees what you have written?)

Respect is the creation of an atmosphere wherein success is encouraged, failures are celebrated as necessary.*

Anthony J. Cedoline

---

* Anthony J. Cedoline, *The Effect of Affect*, San Rafael, CA: Academic Therapy Publications, 1977.

SHELLY AND MISS TIPTON MEET FOR THE FIRST ONE-TO-ONE SESSION

Before Miss Tipton can say anything, Shelly begins, "I was wondering if you were going to talk to me today like you promised. And I suppose you're going to scold me because I wouldn't share the swing with Brooke."

Miss Tipton says, "Let's start over again. I'm glad to see you. I've been looking forward to spending some time with you. These sessions are not for scoldings, Shelly. They are to help you learn that you are special to me. I want to get to know you better."

"I am not going to say much. My dad says that women are gossipy, and I'm not going to be like that."

Miss Tipton reassures her that a gossip talks about other people, and that during their time together they will share about themselves. She picks up the Activities Pages and selects several items to discuss.

"Shelly, I want to read you some interesting questions, and we can discuss your answers. This is not a test. There are no right or wrong answers." She selects the items about promises and secrets.

Shelly doesn't seem interested. "I'd rather twirl than talk," she says.

"You're a fine twirler, Shelly, but I want to make sure that you understand about my promise to you to be your friend. And I need to tell you that I can be trusted not to share what you tell me."

Shelly insists on talking about twirling. "I wore this skirt today because it's my best twirling skirt. My Barbie doll has a skirt in the same color. Do you like it? Want to see me twirl again?"

Miss Tipton suggests, "Let's make a plan. You can twirl three times and then we'll talk. Maybe you'd like to hear about me when I was little. I had a Barbie, too, but she didn't have a dancing skirt. She had clothes for school."

They follow the plan. Shelly doesn't talk about herself. She listens halfheartedly to Miss Tipton's stories. Then she gets up abruptly and says, "The other girls in this class keep secrets from me. I hate them."

There is no response from the teacher.

"If we're going to be here together, I'm going to tell you all the mean things those kids do to me."

Patiently, Miss Tipton answers, "I'm interested in anything you want to tell me. I hope that soon you will trust me enough to talk about yourself."

As they get ready to walk out the door together, Shelly continues her reports on the other girls in the class. "No one likes me," she adds—as if proud of that fact rather than wistful or soft.

Miss Tipton picks up on the remark. "I like you, Shelly. I'm looking forward to seeing you in two days, at the same time."

The child pushes in front of the teacher and leaves without saying goodbye.

(Stories continue on page 32)

COMMITMENT, CARING, AND CONFIDENTIALITY

Directions: Read the questions. Fill in the blanks.

Reminders:
There are no right or wrong answers.
Handwriting and spelling don't count.
All answers are confidential.

A commitment is a promise. What other words can you think of that mean the same thing?

_____

_____

_____

Not all promises can be kept. For example, a dad promises to take his children to the zoo on a Saturday afternoon. Unexpectedly, he has to work. He explains this to the family.
How do you think the children feel? _____

_____

How do you think Daddy feels? _____

Should the mother, an aunt, or friend take them to the zoo instead?

_____

Trust is an important word. Children will say, "He's my buddy. I can trust him to be my friend—even if I'm feeling weird."
Whom do you trust the most? _____

Who trusts you? _____

Do you think it is easier to trust children or grownups? _____

Why? _____

_____

If someone gives away your secret, chances are you will get mad. Have you ever had

someone tell one of your secrets? _____

Did you get mad? _____

What did you do? _____

_____

What you tell the grownup will be safe in a Trust Building Program, unless it has to do with abuse and then the grownup has to, by law, tell someone who can help. This law was passed to help prevent people from getting hurt. What do you think about this law?

_____

_____

A Confidence Building Program helps students learn to feel *confident* about themselves. They have to be encouraged by someone who cares. They can learn to encourage *themselves* to feel confident, too. In what ways would you like someone to encourage you?

_____

_____

_____

_____

_____

_____

_____

_____

ROGER AND MRS. SNYDER MEET FOR THE FIRST ONE-TO-ONE SESSION

Roger arrives on time and waits for Mrs. Snyder to ask him to sit down.

"You said I could talk about anything. Well, I want to talk about that teacher I had last year. She didn't like me. She would say nice things to everyone in the class, but she didn't mean them. One day I heard her tell somebody, 'This class is a drag. These kids are driving me up the wall,' and that afternoon she told us how great we were. Why do teachers do that?"

"That's a hard question to answer, Roger. I don't know the teacher and besides, maybe she was just having a 'down day.' We all have down days once in a while. Are you afraid that I might do the same thing?"

"I dunno," Roger confesses.

Mrs. Snyder goes on to talk about promises and confidentiality. Roger is sad. "No one ever promises me anything. I remember my dad once promised to get me a clock radio, but he forgot. That was when I was in the first grade."

"Roger, I want to tell you again that I promise to meet with you twice a week and that I won't share what you tell me without your permission."

Then, from the Activities Pages she reads a story about the dad who couldn't take his children to the zoo. Roger says, "I'll bet they stayed mad for a long time. My sister doesn't stay mad when things happen to her, but I *do*. You probably don't know it, but my dad drinks too much and maybe that's why he doesn't keep his promises."

"I've noticed that sometimes you act mad, Roger, when I sense that you're really sad instead. People do that, you know." She shares, with him, the Struggles Chart that she has filled in and explains that it is a record to help her remember signs of unhappiness or fear that she has noticed.

Roger is curious. "Do you fill these out for other kids?"

"Yes, at different times. I'm certain that soon I'll write down notes that show you are happier at school."

"I hope so," Roger admits. She offers him some blank Struggles Charts to fill in, but he declines.

The teacher tells Roger about affirmations. "That's for other kids, not me," the boy protests. Mrs. Snyder prompts him to think of three nice things to say about himself. Reluctantly, he comes up with, "I deserve to have friends. I deserve to be told that I am not dumb," and, quietly, he adds, "I deserve these meetings with you."

"I like that," his teacher says as the boy gets up to leave.

TIM AND MR. ATKINS MEET FOR THE FIRST ONE-TO-ONE SESSION

Tim looked forward to meeting with Mr. Atkins and stood at his door to await his arrival. "You're an early morning man, Tim," Mr. Atkins said, opening the door to his office and putting his books on top of his desk.

"Not usually, Mr. Atkins, but I'm kinda curious about this plan. I suppose you'll make me read stuff but I hope not."

The teacher reassures Tim that they can read things over together. He introduces Tim to the Struggles Chart and the Activities Pages. Tim is interested in both documents. He comments about several notes on the chart—he hadn't realized that he was unfriendly to so many children. Mr. Atkins offers Tim some blank charts to fill in, but Tim says it is too soon. Maybe in a week or so he'd try it. The stories and questions on the Activities Pages intrigue him.

"Nobody makes promises to me and I don't make promises to anybody else. That's the best way. Then nobody is disappointed," Tim says.

Mr. Atkins corrects him. "I promised not to share what you tell me and to carry out our plan twice a week, didn't I?"

"I forgot about that," Tim admits.

They discussed the words *commitment* and *confidentiality, trust* and *loyalty,* Mr. Atkins talks a bit about his boyhood. He didn't have visual problems but he had asthma. He was afraid to go places for fear he'd have an attack and not be close to a hospital. He couldn't stay overnight with his cousins or at a friend's house. His mother was very protective and watched over him constantly.

"Boy, it's different at my house," Tim says. "My mom never asks me how I feel. When I'm sick, she goes to work and says she'll call on the phone to see how I am. One time she didn't call until four o'clock in the afternoon. I could have been dead."

The teacher reminds him that he is perfectly capable of using the phone to call her and that people do get absorbed in their work and forget. "I'm going to have to work hard to convince you that you are important to me, Tim. But we're on our way—and that's what counts."

Quite unexpectedly, Tim becomes quiet and seems depressed. When questioned, he replies, "I guess I don't believe you. I like you, but I don't believe you. Maybe I'll never believe I'm important to somebody else."

Mr. Atkins introduces affirmations. He persuades Tim to say, "I deserve to be special to someone." Tim repeats the words. His voice is empty—his emotions flat. At least the Trust Building Program is underway.

MARY AND MRS. BRYCE MEET FOR THE FIRST ONE-TO-ONE SESSION

Mary appears arrogant as she enters the office. "If I'm going to be the leader in this program, there are some things I want to know. How come you chose me? Will you tell my mom? Will there be anything in my records about coming and talking to you? And what's my problem anyway?"

Mrs. Bryce answers each of her questions. She assures her that she will not inform her mother unless Mary requests it, because seeing students in private is a routine responsibility for counselors. No notation will appear on her records, and as for Mary's "problem," they will decide, together, where Mary can use support, encouragement, and direction. Mary seems relieved.

Mary explains that she doesn't want someone to act like her mother— no "guardian angel." "I'm big enough to make my own decisions. Just look around. There are a lot of kids who are having a tough time. I'm okay. Some kids I know have been raped or are in real messes at home. I'm not. I'm just fed up with school and with my family."

Mrs. Bryce shows her the Struggles Chart. Mary agrees to fill one in but has misgivings about its value. When they look over the Activities Pages about *commitment and confidentiality*, Mary laughs. "Teen kids don't keep secrets. Everybody knows who is cool. It's rad to let others know that you'd like to have some guy as a boyfriend. The whole class knows it—even the guy."

Mary and the counselor have a serious talk about choosing friends and peer pressure. Mrs. Bryce makes sure she doesn't sound preachy. It is an enjoyable few minutes for both of them.

After learning about affirmations, Mary prepares to leave. She says she thinks affirmations sound phony, but she'll think about trying them. "Saying nice things about myself is not my thing," she comments as she picks up her books and leaves.

STEP TWO
LIMITS ARE SAFETY ZONES FOR EVERYONE

Background

Children Who Hurt need to understand limits. They often protest rules. They may regard limits as evidence that an adult is just being bossy and really doesn't care. They need to learn that limits are helpful—they keep children from getting into trouble and prevent misunderstandings. There are limits in every family, every school, every clinic, every organization. Some are too strict and arbitrary. Some are lax or unenforceable. If parents fail to set limits, their children feel anxious and unprotected. Children need to learn limits about what they can say or do with other people. This is called self-control.

Some children in Trust Building Programs ask to have some rules bypassed or changed just for them. Others believe that meeting alone with a counselor or teacher means that they will get all kinds of help or favors that their classmates won't get. From the beginning, a child must know that there are rules and limits within a Trust Building Program. Some are determined by the adult; others are negotiated.

Nonnegotiable Limits Limits that *cannot* be changed are called *nonnegotiable*. They are rules for all students. These include:

(1) laws set by state and federal authorities—for instance, *reporting policies in cases of suspected child abuse.*

(2) district limits such as *the school calendar, testing programs, dress code, and social codes* which are set by the Board of Education. These may also include how students are punished if they get in trouble.

(3) limits in a school set by the principal and the teachers.

Review the Important Policies Relevant to a Trust Building Program

- No one is allowed to hurt him- or herself or anyone else.

- The adult will not share anything about the child without the child's knowledge and/or permission.

- There will be no one-to-one sessions for anyone under the influence of drugs or alcohol. (This applies to older students.)

Develop a Policy About Money and Gifts In the materialistic society in which our children are growing up, gifts, money especially, frequently represent acceptance. Kids think, "If people give me something, then they like me." Children Who Hurt may request—even demand—pencils, money, food, books, makeup, and the like.

It is suggested that you state that you will not lend or give money. Tell the child that you have worked with many girls and boys and that you have found this to be a safe policy. Otherwise, if the child requests money and you refuse to get involved, there may be some misunderstanding or unnecessary feelings of rejection.

As a token of your caring, you may occasionally give candy or a piece of fruit. Many times children want to take home a finger painting or crayon sketch that they made during a session. These are not considered gifts. Notes of encouragement may be beneficial.

If a child brings you a gift, this may represent an important break-through. The giving of a gift may be the *first* indication of a willingness to be close to an adult—a first display of trust. It is usually wise to accept the gift. At the same time, be certain to say that your devotion and commitment are there regardless—that you really care anyway.

The Adult Will Not Discuss Other Members of the Faculty.

Children Who Hurt become master manipulators. Bill may be angelic when he is with you, but he misbehaves in Mr. Jones' classroom and acts out in a different way with Miss Brown or Mrs. Karlton. His teachers may feel disgusted, frustrated, amused, or angry. Each adult responds differently. The assorted reactions reestablish for Bill that the world of adults is indeed an unsafe place to be. You cannot influence how other adults will respond to Bill's antics or his attitude or unwillingness to study. You have set a policy—a limit. You will *not* intervene on Bill's behalf. Your work is child-focused, and may need to focus on Bill's need to be provocative and to create turmoil. You can be an empathetic listener and per-haps help Bill recognize his self-defeating habits.

No Promises About Transferring Student

Bill may push, "If you really want me to talk with you, then get me out of Mr. Jones' math class." Deferring to such a demand would be a serious mistake. The Trust Building Program is one between you and the child, and includes no one else. What Bill does with Mr. Jones is not your concern. If you arrange to have Bill transferred out of Mr. Jones' math class *this* week, then *next* week, Bill may want to be out of Miss Brown's science class and then off the bus that Miss Hornsby drives.

It is unprofessional to share, with the child, your negative opinions of fellow members of the staff or faculty. Perhaps Mr. Jones *is* a pain in the neck. He hasn't cracked a smile since last spring vacation. You're glad you're not in his math class. Mr. Jones may be having all kinds of personal problems or may be taking care of his mother who is ill. You do not have to make excuses for colleagues or give out such information. Mr. Jones can share, with Bill, what he wants him to know.

Even though Children Who Hurt may be locked into angry, nonproduc-tive relationships with an adult, *the children themselves are solely responsible for their own behavior.* They are responsible for all changes. They can learn to manage their behavior—even in a class with a teacher they don't like. They can discuss the problems in one-to-one sessions with you.

Most children involved in a Trust Building Program can learn to tolerate unresponsive adults, sarcasm, or other unpleasant attitudes or difficulties without being destroyed. *The fact that they can talk about problems in your one-to-one session is helpful.* They can learn to accept that you are proud of the adjustments they make. They may be willing to accept that a teacher gets frustrated because of disrespectful or disruptive kids in the class and that teachers want kids to learn.

Teachers are people, too. Kids have to take that into consideration.

Note: As mentioned before, it is not the intention of a Trust Building Program to arrange class transfers. However, there are times when such negotiations make sense—when a transfer is possible and advisable. Determine if it is in the best interest of the child. Is the request on the child's part merely to affirm his or her power, or to be vindictive or uncompromising? *Or is there a student-teacher mismatch that is debilitating to this child*? If so, why imprison a child in a nonnourishing relationship when he or she already hurts? Seek the fairest solution.

It is predictable that a Child Who Hurts will attempt to test you by testing the limits.

Negotiable Limits Negotiation builds respect. When kids are allowed to participate with an adult in the negotiation of limits, it builds their respect for the limits and for the adult.

At the beginning of a Trust Building Program it is advisable to consider negotiating times for one-to-one sessions, rules for phone calls and possible help with academics. As the one-to-one sessions continue, Children Who Hurt become more accepting of limits and controls. This acceptance reflects a growing trust.

Times for One-to-One Sessions

In School. A child is told from the beginning, "We will have short meetings together." This means that there is a limited amount of time. Given schedule considerations, be as flexible as possible but negotiate a plan that includes the time limits. "I prefer to meet Tuesdays from 2:50 to 3:15 and Thursdays before school from 7:55 to 8:15. What suggestions do you have?" In practice, the length of the sessions may vary. A minimum of 12 minutes is recommended. A maximum of 22 to 25 minutes for children under ten is a good idea. Older children can handle longer sessions. (If you can only manage one face-to-face session, fill in with a phone call. See **Rules for Phone Calls** below.)

Non-school Based Programs. If the Trust Building Program is being used by mentors, youth leaders, 4–H leaders or other adults who work with children, two weekly face-to-face, one-to-one sessions may not be possible. *However two weekly contacts can be planned and one-to-one sessions woven into workshops, meetings, excursions, or the like.* One contact will be made in person and one by phone. Talk about this ahead of time—even to the point of saying, "We'll make jelly from 1 to 1:30 and have our private meeting from 1:30 to 1:55." Then follow the recommended pattern for one-to-one sessions during that scheduled time. A mentor may invite a child to the movies, a Big Brother and child may go to a ball game, a 4–H supervisor may help shear sheep or make jelly. "Alone time" should not be confused with a designated one-to-one session. Some outings should be just for fun.

Rules for Planned Phone Calls (to fill the recommended pattern of the twice-a-week contacts) The designated time shall be respected and the time limit followed. Follow the pattern of the one-to-one session as best you can—such as starting with a warm greeting: "I've been looking forward to talking to you today," and so forth. Some children may talk more freely on the phone than they do when you're in the same room.

There are two possible problems that may arise. The first has to do with family interference. Be sure to ask the children if they can talk openly or if they feel inhibited because others may be listening. If this is the case, arrange another time to call or have the child call you when appropriate.

The second problem could be the use of the Struggles Chart or Activities Pages. You would have to read the items aloud rather than look over the items or questions together. This can be time consuming or confusing. You may decide not to bother using the charts or activities over the phone unless you select certain questions to discuss ahead of time.

Kids enjoy using the phone, and talking to you can be a positive, productive aspect of any Trust Building Program. Even a stilted phone call reaffirming your concern is better than a prolonged lapse in your work together.

Rules for Unplanned Phone Calls Phone calls may be necessary for some children who face frequent crises and need to talk to you immediately. Some children need to be in touch by phone for reassurance and support.

One adult may extend an open-ended offer, "Call me any time you need to. I know it's hard to study or go to sleep if your mom and dad are fighting or you are worried because your sister didn't come home."

Another adult might say, "I am available until 10 p.m. Try not to call me after that unless there is an emergency."

Discuss Your Limits With the child's help, structure what feels right to you and what you predict will meet his or her needs. You are not competing with any other adult. Programs will differ. Your arrangements with children should be a private matter.

Classroom teachers should not be involved with more than two Trust Building Programs at a time, so that they are not overburdened with appointments and phone calls. Children can be reluctant to phone counselors or teachers, and this matter must also be addressed.

Should you have Trust Building Sessions in the child's home? There are many complicated reasons why home sessions are not recommended. It is more complex than just parental interference. Children may be embarrassed by living conditions, sibling problems, neighbor interference, etc.

Children Who Hurt may feel insecure, inept, unworthy, inadequate, or powerless. However, each has a seed of wellness—a bit of self-acceptance. One goal of a Trust Building Program is to discover that seed and help it grow and flourish. Limits protect the growing seedling.

Limits there must be. Limits keep a Trust Building Program manageable and relieve adult anxiety. You will not find yourself "in over your head."

Reminders for Adults A Trust Building Program requires empathy. By maintaining emotional distance, however, the adult ensures self-protection. There is a vast difference between sympathy and empathy. The sympathetic adult identifies with the children, suffers with them and becomes emotionally involved in their successes and failures. The adult who empathizes understands the children and accepts them with warmth and love.

Strategies for One-to-One Sessions

Purpose: To describe the structure and restrictions of a Trust Building Program and negotiate some limits together with the child. To define how far a counselor or teacher can go on behalf of a child and to prevent manipulations. To provide an opportunity for the child to talk about authority and rules. To explain that limits are a deterrent to impulsiveness—external controls that enhance the development of internal controls.

Directions: Explore the concept and use of limits and rules. Express these ideas in your style. Use your own vocabulary.

Important Adult Statements to Express to a Child

- Limits mean that I care. Limits help people feel secure. Everybody has to obey limits—to stop at stop signs or for school busses when kids are getting on or off. Sometimes limits seem unfair. Limits are an important part of the Trust Building/Confidence Building Plan.

Tell the children the limits or rules of one-to-one sessions. They are free to:

- tell anything they want to tell.

- ask any kind of questions they want or need to ask.

- use dirty words if necessary to describe feelings. This is for release of anger. (The adult must not judge or condone.)

In the Trust Building Program, the child is **not** free to

- hurt him- or herself or others.

- destroy property. (The adult can find things for the child to hit or tear up if needed.)

In the Trust Building Program, the adult is **not** free to

- disclose the child's revelations without the child's knowledge/ permission.

Other rules that must be followed

- The child still must attend classes.

- There will be a time limit on each session. Extra meetings may be negotiated if necessary.

- If there comes a time when it is important for a counselor or teacher to talk to others on behalf of the child, this must be discussed with the child beforehand. As a rule, a teacher must not talk to other teachers if that other teacher has hurt a child's feelings or made a child feel embarrassed or scared. Most teachers do not want to hear criticisms about how they work with any of their students. A Trust Building Program focuses on changes that the child can make. Counselors may need to inform a teacher about something traumatic that may have happened in order to have the teacher be sensitive to the child's needs. Tell the child beforehand that you will be sharing the information.

- In order to avoid confusion in a Trust Building Program, the adult must not give or lend money to children. Occasionally, it is appropriate to give food, candy, or encouraging notes.

*Hold to limits even if a child makes accusations
or tries manipulations such as:*

- If you really like me, then you'll lend me some money. I've got to have money to buy my mom a present.

- You're chicken. I can't believe you won't write an excuse for me.

- If you cared, you'd let me stay at your house.

- If you really liked me, you'd give me a better grade.

- Why don't you make the other kids play with me?

At times, use your sense of humor when you respond to such pleas. "I've figured out that you're trying to push me. Sorry—it won't work."

Promote Discussion

Select items from Activity 2–1.

End of the Session

Set the time for the next one-to-one session.

End with an optimistic, personal statement: "I'm looking forward to seeing you. I'm sure we can. . . ."

Use affirmations. Repeat instructions as often as necessary.

MISS TIPTON AND SHELLY DISCUSS RULES AND LIMITS

Shelly comes out of the girl's restroom and returns to her classroom. All of a sudden she yells at Megan who is getting a book off the shelf. "Megan, I *hate* you and all your friends." Then Shelly walks over to Miss Tipton. With tears in her eyes, she announces, "And I hate you, too." The group is quiet. They wait to hear what Miss Tipton has to say.

Miss Tipton stands in front of the child and doesn't say anything. It is the first time she has seen Shelly out of control. Shelly screams, "Didn't you hear what I said? I said 'I hate you.' "

Miss Tipton responds quietly, "I hear a little girl who is very sad or very afraid of something. I hear a little girl saying, 'Please pay attention to me.' I

(Continued on page 44)

LIMITS ARE SAFETY ZONES FOR EVERYONE

Directions: Read the questions. Fill in the blanks.

Reminders:
There are no right or wrong answers.
Handwriting and spelling don't count.
All answers are confidential.

There is always a reason for a limit or rule even if we may not agree or we think it is dumb.

Most kids dislike being told what to do. How do you feel when someone tells you

what to do? _____

_____

_____

_____

What are the reasons behind:
fire drills?   curfews?   finishing assignments?
stop signs?   tardies?   attending classes?
not being allowed to leave school grounds without permission?

_____

_____

_____

_____

Kids have to deal with limits every day. Schools have many rules.
Be on time.   Don't bring any knives to school.
Hand your papers in on time.   Don't hit.
Don't get on any bus except your own.
Which ones do you think are fair? _____

_____

_____

_____

If you could change any of the rules, which ones would they be and what changes

would you make? Why? _____

_____

_____

Parents are not allowed to abuse their kids. It is against the law. What do you think of those laws? Do you think that they do any good?

Imagine a place where there are *no* limits. What would it be like?

How would it feel to live there?

Do you think children would be happy in such a place?

> **Adults have to respect many rules or laws. They have to make a report if a child is being physically or sexually abused. Even if such a report is necessary, the trust building program can go on.**

also hear a little girl saying, 'I need you to help me so I don't lose control.' "
She looks into the child's eyes.

Shelly clenches her fists and hits Miss Tipton on the leg. The teacher takes hold of her wrist to prevent her from hitting again. "Shelly, hitting is not okay. You are not allowed to hurt yourself or anyone else. If you need to hit or throw, we'll find something. Everyone gets angry. Everyone has a way of showing that they are mad—but there are limits, Shelly, and one is *no hitting*." Miss Tipton continues to hold the child's wrist. Shelly's fingers relax and Miss Tipton gently rubs the child's arm in a reassurring way.

Later, in their one-to-one session, Miss Tipton said, "The word *hate* is a strong word and it tells me a lot about you. Lots of people use that word when they don't mean it at all. Did you think that I would end our Trust Building Program if you hit me and told me that you hate me? No, Shelly, that won't happen."

Shelly confesses, "One time I hit my grandmother and she said, 'Oh, sweetie, don't do that.' That was when I was little. I don't get mad at her very often. When I do tell her that I hate her, she cries, and that makes me feel bad. I get all mixed up about people. Lots of time I want to hit other people but I don't always do it."

Miss Tipton and Shelly talk about limits and rules. Shelly says she likes to play teacher so that she can make up the rules. When she plays with her cousins, she likes to trick them and change the rules so that they get mad. When they get mad, they begin to hit.

Miss Tipton repeats the statement she made in class. "Hitting is *not okay*. That's a rule. That's a *limit*."

MRS. SNYDER AND ROGER DISCUSS RULES AND LIMITS

(Mrs. Snyder and Roger have met four times. Each time Roger is reassured that confidentiality is basic to trust. Roger understands, though the following incident *almost* destroys his budding feelings of trust.)

"Guess what my Roger did today?" Mrs. Snyder exclaims in front of all the teachers in the lounge. "When Susie slipped on the ice and hurt her ankle getting off the bus, Roger handled the situation. He took off his coat, wrapped her up, kept the other kids away, and called for help." Some of the other teachers in the lounge express surprise. "He can't always be a problem," his art teacher says good-naturedly.

Within a few minutes, the bell rings and Roger walks into the art room. He is greeted warmly. "Mrs. Snyder told me that you helped Susie today. Good work."

Roger's face shows dismay. "Why were they talking about me?" he mused. "I wonder what else they said." Now he feels suspicious and confused He had heard Mrs. Snyder promise "confidentiality." Maybe she's not trust-worthy after all. She had broken one of the rules of the Trust Building Program. Now he is concerned that Mrs. Snyder will tell about his home problems that he has described to her.

If Mrs. Snyder wanted to tell the art teacher about Roger, she should have asked him first. He should have had a clear choice. Mrs. Snyder should have asked, "May I tell Miss Bright what you did this morning? I'd really like her to know." Roger might have answered either, "Yeah, it's okay" or "No, please don't. It's no big deal." *Mrs. Snyder should then defer to his wishes* in order to maintain her credibility. Suppose Roger had said, "Please do not tell," and Mrs. Snyder shared with other teachers against Roger's wishes. This could have injured the growing trust relationship. Roger's negative ideas about adults would have been reinforced again because Mrs. Snyder did not respect his choice.

Roger asks Mrs. Snyder, "Why were you talking about me?" She reassures him that several teachers had seen what happened and commented about his thoughtfulness; she merely added to their nice remarks. He accepts this. The developing Trust Building Program has not been destroyed, and Mrs. Snyder has now had clearer direction on how to get Roger's permission to avoid future possible misunderstandings.

Roger had understood a *rule*. He believed that Mrs. Snyder did not respect a rule that she had promised to keep. This bothered him a lot, justifiably.

Another limit (or rule) is tested when Roger wants to borrow some money from Mrs. Snyder. He doesn't know how to ask. He has never asked to borrow money before, but next week is his mom's birthday and he wants to buy her something or pay to do something special with her. He thought about taking her to McDonalds. When the one-to-one session begins, he appears disinterested.

"I'm glad to see you, Roger. What's been happening? I was talking to Mr. Clemens in the hall and found out that you are trying out for the school play. I'm glad to know about that."

Once again he asks, "Why were you talking about me?"

Mrs. Snyder hurries to reassure him, "Mr. Clemens read me the list of all the students who tried out. You were only one name on the list. Are you still worried that I might tell someone about your dad's drinking problem?"

Roger looks sullen. "Yeah, I guess I am. But I do hope I get a part in the play. Hey, you could lend me some money—I could take my mom to a movie for her birthday and watch the people act. Could you lend me five dollars?"

Mrs. Snyder sorts things out. "Roger, I don't lend money to children. I'm glad you want to remember your mom's birthday. I can help you make something for her. Your idea about the movies doesn't sit right with me. You can watch people act on TV. I believe that when someone lends money it can create problems. If I lend you money, you might think, 'How come she only loaned me five dollars instead of ten? I guess she doesn't like me very much.' That would be all wrong. I like you a lot. You are special to me. I just don't want our relationship getting mixed up with money matters."

Roger shrugs his shoulders. "My mom probably wouldn't appreciate a present from me anyway. Can we talk about something else?"

Mrs. Snyder suggests they could make a small book and paste his school picture in it. This doesn't interest Roger either. She makes three other suggestions.

Roger says, "I really would like to *buy* her something and I don't have any money. Why can't you change your mind? If I'm special to you, you could lend me five dollars. I'll pay you back."

"Let's get this clear, Roger. I do not give children material presents or lend money. That's not what *trust* is all about. People think *things* are important because they see so many commercials on TV and some parents give their kids a lot of money or presents to make up for *not* giving them much love and attention."

"I don't get either," Roger complains. In a soft voice, he adds, "You're the only one who listens to me. I guess you're right. I'll draw her a picture. Maybe she'll like that. She'll probably put it somewhere so nobody will see it anyway. She puts my sister's pictures on the refrigerator door. My sister is in kindergarten. Her pictures always have a tree and a rainbow."

Roger and Mrs. Snyder go on to talk about ways that people show that they care. "Do you think my dad cares for my mom?" Roger wants to know.

"I have no way of knowing about that, but I'm glad that you are learning to express your feelings. I had to work at that, too. I never saw my father and mother touch each other. My father would pat me on the head when he said 'goodnight.' He never kissed me. I learned to touch and kiss people from my best friend's mother who was a 'touching' lady. I'm glad you will let me pat you on the head."

Before leaving the session, Roger says, "I'll make Mom a picture and write a poem. Maybe she'll like that."

"Good thinking. Let's have an affirmation before you go."

Roger doesn't hesitate one minute. "I deserve a pat on the head."

"Right on!" Mrs. Snyder replies.

MR. ATKINS AND TIM DISCUSS RULES AND LIMITS

Tim wants Mr. Atkins to let him be a team captain and choose the players. He has met with Mr. Atkins four times and accepts that his teacher really likes him. Before class, he announces in a demanding way, "If you want me to meet with you again, you'll let me be a captain." Mr. Atkins makes his point—in a hurry, "We have rules about picking captains in this class. We go by last name, alphabetical order. We are in the G's—and you, young man, are a K. No such luck. A rule's a rule—that's it."

Tim looks sullen. Mr. Atkins takes him aside. "Your bargaining about our one-to-one talks is not cool. I'm going to pretend I didn't hear you" and with that, he walks away. Tim is relieved. He really didn't mean it. Mr. Atkins is aware that Tim's attachment to his mother is tenuous. He wants Tim's attachment to him to be reassuring, yet he must follow procedures that the kids consider fair. He wants to model fairness for Tim. In one of their first talks Tim had said, "I don't think that it's fair that my mom spends more time with her boyfriend than she spends with me." This statement had given Mr. Atkins some important clues.

That afternoon, when they meet for their next one-to-one session, Tim shows up holding his notebook against his chest. Mr. Atkins can see a magazine showing below the notebook. He is curious but doesn't ask any questions. Before long Tim volunteers, "I wanted to show you a cartoon my friend brought me. I guess it's kinda dirty." He puts it on the desk in front of the teacher, then turns his back and moves toward the window.

It is indeed a dirty cartoon. Mr. Atkins hands it back to Tim and says, "I think some cartoons like that are pretty funny. Others don't amuse me at all. I'm glad you can trust me enough to share it with me. Thanks."

Tim admits, "I didn't have anyone else to show it to and I thought you might like it. Do you read that magazine?"

Mr. Atkins doesn't answer right away. Then he says, "I don't discuss my private life with anyone, Tim. It wouldn't be professional to go into details about that."

"But when I have questions, I don't have anyone to ask. That neighbor boy is as dumb as I am, and my mom would freak out if I asked her some of the things I want to know." He pauses. "Mr. Atkins, what is 'The Clap'? Is it the same as AIDS?"

The teacher answers the boy's direct questions for a few minutes, reiterating several times, "I realize you don't have any males in your household." He reminds Tim that he, too, had been a fatherless boy.

They go over the Struggles Chart that Tim has filled out over the past several days.

"Glad to see you ate lunch with those two guys in the cafeteria. I remember when you preferred to eat alone."

"Me? Alone? You're joking!"

"No, I'm not. When kids are sarcastic, they scare people away and that's what you used to do. Happy to see that you figured out what to do. You're a smart kid, Tim. You're learning about the real world. If you are being rude to your mom after all these years, I'll bet she's tired of it, too. No wonder she likes to spend a lot of time with her boyfriends."

"I'm not so sure about that, Mr. Atkins, but I'll think about it."

Tim tucks his magazine behind his notebook as he heads out the door. "Thanks for seeing me," he says. "I'm glad you asked me to do this Trust Building thing with you. By the way, I'm sorry about that 'captain stuff' that I pulled."

"How about an affirmation before you leave? Mr. Atkins asks. Tim's eyes twinkle "I deserve a friend like you." The two smile warmly.

MRS. BRYCE AND MARY DISCUSS RULES AND LIMITS

Mary walks into Mrs. Bryce's office and hands her a modified completed Struggles Chart and says, "I tried to fill this thing out. It's wasn't easy. I've had it two weeks. I don't think the chart is worth anything at all, Mrs. Bryce. It's a waste of time—but here it is."

Together they read the entries.

Date	What happened?	How Often	Other notes
11/18	Told Patty to get lost. She's a snob.	2	
11/19	Helen was in a bad mood Told her "See you later."	1	Helen is moody a lot. I like her hair. She is friendly to me if any boys are around.
11/19	Ran in the hall. Sent to the office.	1	Another dumb school rule.
11/21	Helped Jane with her homework.		Had a good time today. Don't know why.
11/22	Saw Mrs. Bryce today.		It's okay to have someone to talk to.
11/24	Mom made me so mad, I cried.	2	I hate being the kid who gets nothing. Wish I could split.
11/27	Mr. Ryan is a creep. I hate him. He insults kids. I won't look at him face-to-face.	A lot	I gotta get out of this class.

Mrs. Bryce praises her, "This is good, Mary. Thanks for doing what I asked you to do. It's great that you helped Jane with her homework, and I like your note about meeting with me. That problem with Mr. Ryan—we've talked about that. What's happening with your mom?"

"She *never* listens to anything I say. Whenever I tell her about something bad that happens, she says, 'It's not as bad as you think.' Sometimes she says, 'You'll outgrow it. All girls get emotional when they are teenagers,' and that makes me mad. You are the only one who listens to me."

They are both quiet for a while.

Mary speaks up, "When my report card came the other day, we had a fight. Mom is never satisfied with anything I do, and yet, if I ask her to help me, she won't do it. She had the nerve to tell me she'd helped enough kids with homework and that I'm smart—so I can do it by myself. She doesn't care what I do.

"The other night I was home alone after my friends left. There was a strange noise outside and I was scared. I called 911. I didn't know what else to do. Well, the cops were there when she got home and she was mad. It seems like she's always mad at me. She's not much of a mother. If I *really* got in trouble, I wonder what she'd do. She probably wouldn't even care if I dropped out of school."

"It sounds to me as if you want your mother to be more involved in what you do. Do you know what I mean by that?"

"Yeah," Mary says. "I guess so, *but* I don't want her telling me how to fix my hair or how long I can talk on the phone."

"When you add up all your complaints, it seems as if you feel you are taking care of yourself. Maybe you want somebody to tell you, 'This is okay.' or 'This is not okay.' That's called *making rules or setting limits*—just like every school has limits, and so do I—right here in this office."

"Yeah," Mary says, "I remember that you said something about nobody can hurt anybody else when they meet with you. Well, it hurts me when my mom doesn't care what I do."

Mrs. Bryce answers, "I want to help you, Mary. I can't fix things up with your mom. If you *really* want her to set some limits, tell her. But, Mary, it's my impression you don't like to be told what to do. Do you want your mother to get bossy or set limits only because that would show that she cares?"

"Well, no, but I wish she'd find *some way* to show it," Mary answers.

"She tells you that you are smart, Mary. I think that means she has faith in your common sense and decisions."

"I suppose so," Mary agrees.

They talk about mom-daughter communication. Mary repeats that she feels unwanted. She admits that when she was little, she was teased and called a "spoiled brat" because she could do almost anything she wanted to do.

"That was like having no limits, wasn't it?" her counselor interjects.

"I never thought about that. Anyway, I wasn't happy. My dad thought I was pretty, but my mom never said anything nice to me. My brothers and sisters said I was a pest. My dad wasn't around very much. When he did come home, he'd bring me a present. He never brought Mom anything. Maybe she was jealous and that's why she treats me the way she does."

They go over her Struggles Chart again and then discuss some items from the Activities Pages. Mary smiles when she says, "I'd change that No Smoking rule here at school. I think kids should be allowed to smoke if they want to." Mrs. Bryce disagrees. "You know that smoking can cause cancer. Why take a chance?"

Mary gives an honest answer: "Because I like it and besides it makes my mother mad." Mrs. Bryce says she tried it once and hated the taste. Before Mary leaves, they confirm their next appointment and make up some affirmations. The girl says she'd like to fill out another Struggles Chart. "I'm not sure why—guess it's something to do when I'm bored in class."

STEP THREE
DEPENDENCY IS IMPORTANT

Background

Children Who Hurt have a history of unfulfilled dependency needs. Many did not get sufficient nurturing. They miss a close emotional bond. They feel that no one cares. Perhaps their parents are emotionally impoverished or have problems that keep them from taking care of the emotional needs of their kids. Unsatisfied dependency needs result in mistrust of adults. Children Who Hurt have learned that adults are not to be trusted. Even young Children Who Hurt are afraid to become dependent because of ongoing disappointments. They become unresponsive or stiff. The dilemma is clear—these children crave dependency and are afraid of it at the same time.

When children are prematurely *cast into a self-sustaining role*—real or imagined—*or feel detached, abandoned or neglected*—they become frightened, hopeless, and sad.

When people have been hurt or feel unwanted, they usually pull away. They become quiet or go off by themselves. They may not answer questions or they may be unfriendly—even to their parents, sisters and brothers, or teachers. In a Trust Building Program, a boy or girl can depend on the grownup to be friendly and caring. This is an important introduction to dependency—a way to counteract feelings of being unwanted.

Indicators of Neediness and Dependency

- needs attention constantly—teacher notes, "always insists that I notice every picture she makes"

- wants to have someone make his or her decisions

- needs to be close, to touch, or hang around

- needs endless encouragement

- drops hints or makes demands for miscellaneous gifts, cards, notes

- asks for help or approval constantly

- extends invitations of all sorts—"I want you to come and live at my house"

- pretends to be helpless

If a child reaches out or expresses, even in a tentative way, a willingness to be close to an adult, this may be marked improvement—a sign that the child is beginning to trust. It is important. Be gentle. For some Children Who Hurt, first indications of dependency should be accepted with little or no discussion. Your attitude and receptivity put the welcome message across.

You cannot persuade a Child Who Hurts to experiment with dependency. It develops after the child believes your commitment.

Dependency may be slow to develop.

In testing out dependency, a child may become very dependent in a very short time. You may be unprepared for this. It needs careful handling.

After the first indicators, you may see a flood of them—a nonstop plea for attention or help. This may become exhausting to you. *This is another reason to limit yourself to two Trust Building Programs at one time.*

Dependency can nurture both the counselor and the child. Many adults gain a sense of importance or increased value as a human being when children appear weak, dependent, or needy. They want to comfort children—give them closeness and warmth when they crave it. These children may become very special to that adult.

The heightened dependency phase of a Trust Building/Confidence Building Program should last approximately three to four weeks for children below the age of eight and four to six weeks for children up to eleven or twelve. Older Children Who Hurt may, however, be less demanding and more wary but need extended time to talk. The content of their one-to-one sessions may have to deal with the emotional swings of the preadolescent years as well as personal problems, and that's a big load.

There is no way to predict when a child will risk dependency or how long the exaggerated dependency demands may last.

A successful moment of dependency may be a first taste of trust.

Strategies for One-to-One Sessions

Purpose: To explain closeness, reliability, and consistency. To describe and discuss indicators of neediness and dependency. To encourage a child to become dependent without censure. To assure children that dependency provides the opportunity to feel taken care of, protected, and safe. To explain that people in caring relationships learn to depend on each other.

Directions: Discuss the importance of dependency. Build a positive attitude toward asking for help and attention. Express these ideas in your own style. Use your own vocabulary.

Explain to the Child the Meaning of the Word "Dependent." The word *depen-dent* means a combination of two ideas: to "rely on" and to "take care of." We know that babies are dependent and cannot take care of themselves. Young people need to depend on others a lot of the time. There are times when grownups want someone to help them or take care of them, or they want others to depend on them.

Share About the People You Depend On. Tell the child about the people you depend on such as friends, husband, wife, or mother. Give examples such as, "I share my private thoughts or worries." "Sometimes I ask for help with my car, or my shopping or house work." "My mother gives me advice about cooking." "My husband takes care of me when I have a cold." "My best friend. . . ."

The following sentences indicate dependency. Read each sentence to the child. Ask the child to put these sentences into different words and discuss what they mean.

- Jason never asks for help. He thinks no one wants to help him or be his friend.

- Mary needs attention constantly. She feels weird if no one is paying attention to her.

- Jim needs to have somebody make his decisions for him.

- Helen wants her desk right next to the teacher's. Helen wants to sit next to her teacher in the circle, too.

- Bud hangs around his teacher whenever he has a chance.

- Louise pretends that she can't do things by herself. She wants someone to help her.

- Whenever Bill does anything, he wants someone to tell him that he did a good job.

- Sue needs to touch her teacher whenever she can. She frequently asks to be patted on her head or her back.

Discuss these sentences. They tell that a person is dependable.

- I will meet you on time.

- Every time, I will tell you how I feel.

- I will be a good friend.

- I will keep your confidences.

- I want you to rely on me to listen to whatever you share.

Ask for a reaction, with examples.

Talk About Broken Appointments.   Broken appointments may be interpreted as a sign that an adult is not dependable. When you cannot keep an appointment, a relationship may be injured. Your absence must be explained carefully. If you know ahead of time that you will be unable to keep an appointment, make every effort to inform the child. If you become ill and must stay home, get your principal to explain why you can't be there for the session. Explanations provided ahead of time are usually accepted more readily than excuses after the fact. Children are self-focused. They will blame themselves if you cannot meet. A child may become convinced that he or she did or said something wrong. "I told her about my dad's drinking. That's why she didn't come today." Such statements reflect a lack of trust.

Promote Discussion

Select items from Activity 3–1.

End of the Session

Set the time for the next one-to-one session.

End with an optimistic personal statement such as, "I'm looking forward to seeing you again. I am sure we can. . . ."

Use affirmations. Repeat instructions as often as necessary.

> **Dependency can be spelled out!**
> **Demonstrated!**
> **Experienced!**
> **Tested!**
> **Enjoyed!**

DEPENDENCY IS IMPORTANT

Directions: Read the questions. Fill in the blanks.

Reminders:
There are no right or wrong answers.
Handwriting and spelling don't count.
All answers are confidential.

Most people like to have someone to depend on and want to have someone depend on
them. Babies depend on grownups. Good friends depend on each other.
In what ways do you depend on:

Your parent(s)?_____

_____

_____

Your teacher?_____

_____

_____

Your friends?_____

_____

_____

Your sisters or brothers or other relatives?_____

_____

_____

Who is dependent on you? How?_____

_____

_____

There is a famous quote by John Donne, "No man is an island unto himself." Do you
believe that? Do you think it means that everybody needs to be close to someone
else?

_____

_____

_____

What about hermits? What makes them want to be a hermit? Are they happy?_____
_____
_____

Do you ever take care of others? How does it make you feel?_____
_____

Are you proud when your best friend tells people that he or she can depend on you to be a good friend even if you have had a fight?_____
_____
_____

Make up a short story about a family where the grandmother has to depend on the other members for money and food. Describe how each person in the family must feel.
_____
_____
_____
_____
_____

One person you don't want to depend on is_____
_____

One person you wish you didn't have to depend on is_____
_____

Reminders for Adults Keep your expectations of the children age-appropriate. This is difficult to do because *Children Who Hurt are too young to be so old, and too old to be so young.* Children who cope by being too independent may not understand your willingness to have them be dependent on you. Being distant from you may be important to their sense of safety.

MISS TIPTON INTRODUCES SHELLY TO DEPENDENCY

Shelly tugs at Miss Tipton's skirt. Miss Tipton leans down. Shelly whispers, "Nobody here talks to me, and I don't like that. I'll be over at the book rack—in case you're looking for me." Miss Tipton is accustomed to Shelly's complaints. "Thanks for telling me where I can find you." Miss Tipton moves toward a group of children who are talking about the new growth on the sweet potato plant.

Shelly flops on the floor and thumbs through some books. She turns over on her back, stares at the ceiling and the bright pictures on the wall. She peeks around the book rack hoping Miss Tipton will come looking for her. Instead, Megan and Janie appear. "What are you doing there, Shelly? Are you sick?" They walk away, not waiting for an answer. Shortly afterward, Bob takes a book off a shelf. He asks the same questions and he, too, walks away.

Shelly's self-talk repeats, "See, nobody cares about me." She ventures out from her hiding place. She looks disgruntled as she approaches the teacher. "I'd like to see you smile," Miss Tipton comments, "and I am looking forward to talking to you after school."

"She's always nice—even when I'm grouchy," Shelly says to herself. "I guess that's what she means when she says, 'You can depend on me.' "

During the one-to-one session, the teacher suggests a game. She will read a word and Shelly will tell her what it means. She selects *cheerful, glad, kind, safe, excited, proud, respect,* and *happy.* Shelly's definitions are accurate, though brief. She doesn't comment or elaborate.

"What do all these words describe, Shelly? Can you figure that out?" The girl asks her teacher to read them again. Shelly looks puzzled. Then she says," "I get it. Those are all *nice* feelings."

"That's right! I chose them to remind you that *you can do things or find things* that make you *feel nice.* I'm concerned when you talk about yourself. I hear words like unhappy, bad, lonely, sad, and dumb."

"I can't help it. Other people are mean to me. You're the only one who is nice to me—except for my grandmother. I know that you will be friendly and that you will listen to me and let me sit next to you."

Miss Tipton says, "I'm glad that you're beginning to feel close to me." Then Miss Tipton changes the subject. "Have you ever noticed that I give every boy and girl a chance to talk? I try to be fair."

Shelly surprises Miss Tipton, "I think you like boys better than girls. I wish I were a boy. Boys are nicer than girls. My daddy is nicer than my mom because he likes me to live with him."

Miss Tipton asks, *"Do you believe that all women and girls may be unfriendly just because your mom doesn't live with you? Is that why you can't depend on girls or women except your grandmother?"*

"I never thought about that," Shelly says. Miss Tipton explains that things that happen to us when we are little can bother us as we get older.

"When I was a little girl, my big brother always told me I was dumb. He told me that he didn't like my socks or the dress I had on. He never liked my hair. I thought I was ugly and that everything I did was wrong. I believed that for a long time.

"Then one day my teacher told me that I had the prettiest hair of any girl in the class. I couldn't believe my ears. I was so surprised that I said, 'Do you mean it?' and of course she did.

"Well, from then on I realized how important a teacher can be to a child. I want to help you think about *nice feelings*, Shelly, and to learn to depend on me to be your friend. You need that, honey."

Miss Tipton gives Shelly a squeeze. Shelly looks up at her and says, "Thanks, Miss Tipton. Maybe, when I grow up, I'd like to be a lady like you."

Miss Tipton reads Shelly some of the questions on the Activities Pages. Shelly thinks that living alone would be better than living with people you don't like or who don't like you. Shelly wants to live alone when she gets older. By then, her grandmother will be too old to have kids around and her father isn't home very much anyway. "I wouldn't have anybody to depend on or who would want to be close to me." Miss Tipton assures her that when she gets older, she might change her mind. She will undoubtedly have new friends to depend on.

MRS. SNYDER INTRODUCES ROGER TO DEPENDENCY

Roger hardly ever smiles. He is jealous when Mrs. Snyder pays attention to other kids, but when she pays attention to him, he acts shy—as if he feels uncomfortable.

After Mrs. Snyder invites him into the Trust Building Program, Roger seems a little less sullen. Several times he starts to approach Mrs. Snyder at her desk but stops. "She probably doesn't want me near her," he mutters to himself. Mrs. Snyder sees this. "Roger, I'd like for you to take some books to the media center for me. They are here on the corner of my desk." She manages a way for him to come close to her. The desk is a safe barrier. Roger takes the books. She repeats this strategy four times. Each day it seems as if he is more comfortable near her. Within a few days, although still protected by the desk, Roger hangs around. Mrs. Snyder doesn't criticize or scold him. There are a lot of smiles exchanged between teacher and child. Roger is beginning to let himself become dependent on Mrs. Snyder. "I can't wait until we talk again" he whispers to her as he goes to lunch.

When they meet in the one-to-one session, Roger is sullen. Mrs. Snyder asks, "What happened to that nice smile I saw before lunch?"

Roger tries to explain. "Well, I asked Jamie to walk around the playground with me and he wouldn't do it. So I told him to get lost."

"Roger, is that what was really bothering you? Could it be that you were not sure how you would feel being alone with me after you had been so friendly? Was there something scary about that? Maybe you haven't learned you can depend on me to be friendly to you."

Roger shakes his head, then cautiously looks up at Mrs. Snyder. "I never thought about that—maybe you're right."

Using the Activities Pages, they talk about dependency. Roger says, "I can't depend on anybody." Then he stops and adds, "except maybe you—a little bit. I think I'll be a hermit when I grow up. I'll have two big dogs, and I'll be happy—I think."

"Perhaps, Roger. I depend on Mr. Snyder in many ways. Some day you might like to be a husband."

"You're *kidding*," he laughs. "I'll take care of myself." Then, surprisingly, he asks, "Could I please move my desk up closer to yours?"

"That's a good idea," his teacher says. Before he leaves, he makes up an affirmation. "I take good care of my books and my toy cars. I deserve a puppy to take care of. Puppies make kids feel good. They are always friendly. I deserve a friendly puppy."

MR. ATKINS INTRODUCES TIM TO DEPENDENCY

Tim thinks Mr. Atkins is a really nice guy. Tim wants to be friendly but he doesn't know how. Every time Mr. Atkins finds a way for Tim to feel special, Tim smiles to himself. If Mr. Atkins asks him a question, he always tells him the truth. Tim doesn't always tell the truth to other people. When Mr. Atkins explains about the Trust Building Program, he says that he will tell the truth and he expects Tim to do the same. Tim has noticed that Mr. Atkins is not critical of him, and every time they say goodbye, Mr. Atkins raises his hand and says, "Give me five!" They clap hands and laugh. Tim tells his mom, "I'm not afraid to talk to Mr. Atkins. I don't feel like a nerd when I'm around him. I'd like to see him every day."

Tim is becoming dependent on his relationship with Mr. Atkins.

In a one-to-one session, Tim asks Mr. Atkins if he would help him decide whether or not to try out for the school play. Mr. Atkin's answer is, "I can't make your decisions for you. If you get a part, that would be great. If you don't, you might still be able to work backstage and help build the set or make props for the play. A play can't go on without the stage crew."

Tim isn't satisfied. He wants more direction (an indicator of dependency). "Do they ever give speaking parts in a play to a kid who has to get special help in school? Will you read over the script with me ahead of time so that maybe I'll get the part? Or should I just skip it?" Tim demonstrates his familiar negative attitude.

"Hold it, Tim. You didn't even hear me when I mentioned working on the stage crew. Besides, I don't like your negative attitude. Whether you get a part in the play or work on the stage crew, think positive, young man—starting now." Mr. Atkins smiles a big smile.

They spend a few minutes discussing what it means to depend on other people and for others to depend on you. Mr. Atkins says that friends give each other encouragement and that they remain friends even if one is in a bad mood.

"I thought that kids are supposed to learn to be independent. Doesn't that mean you're supposed to be able to do everything by yourself?"

"Not at all, Tim. Friends help each other and depend on each other."

"I don't have anybody who depends on me—not even my mom," the boy says thoughtfully. "She says I always forget to do what she asks. Well, her boyfriends can take out the trash, and she can quit being so critical of me."

"Let's just talk about *your* being a dependable friend, and that you can depend on *me* to be here for you." They read items from the Activities Pages.

"Thanks for the discussion, Mr. A. I get it. I'm not a bad kid, and I do deserve friends." He repeats the last sentence over and over as he leaves the room.

MRS. BRYCE INTRODUCES MARY TO DEPENDENCY

Mary has a problem respecting adults. This complicates her relationship with her counselor, Mrs. Bryce. Mary has thirteen years of mistrust to overcome. Her *big* defense is "I can go it alone" and she believes that a grownup who tries to be her friend intends to be critical and bossy. She is not excited about the Confidence Building Program. She is curious. Mary tells one of her friends, "Whenever I meet with Mrs. Bryce, I ask her a bunch of dumb questions. I ask her stuff I already know, and she never gets impatient. She lets me say anything I want."

The one-to-one talks help meet Mary's need for attention. She's beginning to feel a bit secure. Mary is less rude and callous with Mrs. Bryce. She is learning to depend on this relationship which explains why she is less defensive and more relaxed.

In one session, Mary and Mrs. Snyder look at the Activities Pages. *Do you like to take care of others? How does it make you feel?* Mary says, "I don't like to take care of others and I'll tell you why. Nobody ever says 'Thank you.' When my grandmother broke her hip, I fixed her breakfast every day for two weeks. I'd put it on her bed and all she could say was, 'Be quiet. I'm listening to *Good Morning, America.*' I don't want to take care of babies or sick people or even a cat."

Mrs. Bryce says, "When people feel helpless, like your grandmother did, they can be unpleasant. Don't you like babies and little kids?"

"No, I have a lot of nieces and nephews. My mom makes a big fuss over them. The kids don't pay any attention to me."

"What do you do when they come to visit?"

"I go to my room and watch TV. I'm not going to get all sentimental about some little kids—just cause they are in the family."

Mrs. Bryce is not critical. "Maybe you'll change your mind about babies, Mary. I loved taking care of my son, Bobby, when he was little. It made me feel special. My husband felt that way, too. It was a little sad to watch him grow up and become more independent."

"I didn't know you had a kid."

"Yes, he's nine now. I don't mean to sound preachy, Mary, but most everyone needs to depend on someone to love them, and that means they need to show love, too."

"I depend on my friends, Mrs. Bryce, and that's enough for me."

"It's important to love yourself, too, Mary, but you don't stop loving yourself just because you love someone else."

"That sounds like some fancy wedding ceremony, but I get what you mean. I deserve to depend on my friends and that feels good." Mary is quite cheerful for the rest of the session.

STEP FOUR
FACTS HELP CHILDREN COPE

Background

A Trust Building Program is founded on the conviction that facts, plans, expectations, and goals should be explained to children fully. *Children can deal with almost anything if told the truth.* They need facts. They can *handle* facts although they may need to hear repeated explanations. They *respect* people who tell the truth. They *feel respected* when told the facts.

You select a child to enter one-to-one sessions based on observations or facts that you have noted. In forthcoming sessions, you may share these observations with the child. Some are recorded on a Struggles Chart. You will help the child to accept these facts and many others—even though some may be painful. It is advisable to veer in the direction of sharing too many facts rather than withholding any pertinent plans or information.

If a child discovers that you withhold information, the child may confront you. The child may say, "Why didn't you *tell* me that I had to take that test?" or "Why didn't you tell me that my father is never coming back?" "You tell me to tell you what I'm feeling or what I know. Why don't you do the same for me?" These questions express a lack of trust, in the hopes of inciting an honest reply from you.

A Child Who Hurts needs to know plans and expectations ahead of time. Surprises build anxiety in an already-anxious child. Uncertainty feeds the child's feelings of insecurity. The child may anticipate that a nice surprise today may be followed by the announcement of an unpleasant surprise tomorrow. If the child has just endured an unhappy event, she/he may visualize another one unnecessarily. Whenever possible, describe future events realistically.

Too often we avoid mentioning a traumatic episode a child has experienced. *It is a fact of his or her world. The child has had to cope with it.*

When you discuss the facts of a traumatic episode with a Child Who Hurts, there is a possibility that you may be the first person who has been open with him and willing to work with the reality of what happened. You may be the first person who can help the child confront old or current feelings. You may be the first one willing to listen in a nonjudgmental way.

Selected Facts Children May Need Children are self-focused and most of the questions they ask—the facts they seek—pertain to something personal or to their family. They also need impersonal facts about other families in order to understand their own situation. Impersonal facts such as "Most children of divorce blame themselves for the breakup of the family," are objective and businesslike. Children Who Hurt may find impersonal facts reassuring.

Selected facts about divorce, death, drinking and drugs, violent behavior, and the trauma of moving are described below.

Divorce: A Divorce Is a Grownup Decision It usually happens when one partner decides the situation is hopeless. That feeling of hopelessness usually builds over a long period of time—perhaps after years of misunderstandings, fights, or separations. Children experience a deep sense of loss when the family breaks up. This can affect them in many ways for years to come.

Death It takes a long time to recover from the loss of a loved one or even a relative stranger. Some parents and other adults have a difficult time discussing death. Death is final. All people die. When someone dies or is killed, it is not a rejection of a child. A person who commits suicide is almost always displaying personal despair. It is helpful for survivors to talk about the death and about their feelings.

Drinking and Drugs Some people become addicted to alcohol. They are called alcoholics. They cannot control how much they drink or how they behave when they are drunk. They can get help. If one person in a family is an alcoholic, *everyone* is affected. The alcoholic may do or say mean things, may be dishonest, and very inconsistent. This causes confusion and hurt. Children do not cause their parents to drink or use drugs.

Violent Behavior Everyone gets angry, but most people do not show their anger by hurting someone or something. People who hurt others usually have a lot of problems. They may be lonely or drink too much or have a lot of worries or stress. They might have been beaten or abused as a child. People can learn to express anger without hurting others. The people who get hurt are called victims. It takes a lot of hard work and a long time to recover from being a victim, but it is possible.

Moving, Changing Neighborhoods, Changing Schools One out of every ten families in America moves every year.

A child has the right to know why the family is moving—even if the reasons are not happy ones.

A child has the right to select some favorite possessions to take along.

A child may be tired, scared, or upset when starting at a new school and should be encouraged to tell his or her teacher or counselor.

A child should be encouraged to ask new teachers for time to catch up with the rest of the class and to ask for special help.

A child should be encouraged to tell a counselor or teacher if something sad or upsetting happened before the move. Chances are the parents were upset, too, and not able to listen or talk to the child at that time. Some families move frequently and are not in the habit of sharing facts or discussing feelings.

Children need to be reassured that most kids want to be friendly and that there are new friends to be made in every school.

Children can learn that all families have problems to solve that the children cannot repair. A child's responsibility is to learn to manage his or her own behavior, do well in school, and make friends. Counselors and teachers and other caring adults find ways to help children be self-accepting. They often refer to facts such as evidence of a child's wellness as part of the helping process.

Children hate to be lied to. They feel betrayed if they discover they have been told a half-truth. If someone omits a detail, they feel cheated. They feel belittled and excluded when told, "You are too young to understand."

The adult in a Trust Building Program must tell the truth and share facts consistently. Truth builds respect. Children Who Hurt crave respect.

As a therapist, I had some sensitive moments. A nine-year-old child's father, a convicted child molester, was due to be released from the state prison. It was expected that the full story would appear in the paper. I didn't want the child to learn the facts from the media. I felt that the respectful, caring thing to do was to tell him—in the safe environment of a trust relationship. His mother concurred. The youngster was grateful—very grateful. He coped well. He felt he could understand the personal problems his father had had. He felt prepared to face the days ahead.

One child may not believe the facts—the truths he or she is told. Another child may deny them. Children may get angry at you for telling them something they don't want to hear, but the impact of your trustworthiness— displayed as honesty—cannot be compared to any other experience in helping a child learn to trust. It is essential.

No printed word nor spoken plea
can teach young minds what men should be
not all the books on all the shelves
but what the teachers are themselves.
                                                    Anonymous

---

Reminders for Adults Accept that what a child shares with you may open old wounds of *yours*. If what the child shares makes you uncomfortable, share your feelings about the old trauma with a friend or confer with a professional. It is not necessary to tell the child about this issue.

Strategies for One-to-One Sessions

Purpose: To make certain that children understand that adults share facts in order to establish trust. To clarify that when children are told plans and facts, they can anticipate what they will have to do and how they will be expected to behave. To acknowledge that children trust adults who are honest and predictable.

Facts can curtail a need to fantasize or daydream, which may interfere with concentration and learning.

Directions: Relay information about facts. Use your own vocabulary.

Important Statements to Express to a Child

- When I tell you facts or we look them up, it is to provide you with a sense of certainty.

- I will not pretend I don't know what I know or see what I see.

- Based on facts, we can talk about why certain things happen, what needs to be done, and how I can help.

In one-to-one sessions, we will use facts from:

- Struggles Chart notations

- written records,

- information from books, articles

- test results, class work, and what you tell me. We may also refer to my professional or teaching materials.

I will share facts about me.

Secrets frequently damage relationships, and I don't want that to happen to us. I will tell you many things about me.

Distinguish facts from rumors, wishes, half-truths, guesses, or prejudicial remarks.

Help Children Learn to Ask for Facts. Explain that some children want facts about their families, other families, or themselves, and need encouragement to ask for them. They learn how to ask what they want to know in one-to-one sessions. Read the list of **Children's Statements** (Page 65). Ask, "Do any of these statements apply to you?" Discuss the statements or problems the child selects.

The Children's Statements—Pleas for Facts, Information, and Explanations:

- I want to know what happened in my family before I was born. *When I don't know about a situation, I make a lot of guesses* and I keep thinking that everything will turn out bad.

- I need facts about other kids and other families to help me understand what's happening at my house.

- I want information about you. I want facts about all the people who are important in my life.

- Why does my mom drink? Do all moms drink?

- Do kids cause divorces? Will my mom and dad ever be friends?

- After someone dies, how long does it take before a person feels better? Is it okay to cry?

- Do all dads have temper tantrums? Why doesn't my dad just scream at my mom instead of hitting her?

- Why do we have to move so much? Don't my parents know I hate to change schools?

- I need you to explain *how* I can learn.

Based on the child's responses, answer with *facts* that you know. Use impersonal facts about families such as those included in the **Background Section** (Page 61). If not applicable, use explanations such as, "I do not know your mother (or father). I cannot answer that question," or, "Every person is unique. I don't know why your dad. . . ."

Do not promise to make inquiries about family matters although you may want to read whatever records are available. Stay child-focused.

Encourage the child to ask parents, or others, what he or she wants to know. When the child shares with you what he or she has been told, *support feelings and reaffirm the child's positive qualities* that help him or her to cope.

If the child's questions deal with personal learning problems, explain

FACTS HELP CHILDREN COPE:
IT IS IMPORTANT TO KNOW THE TRUTH

Directions: Read information about facts. Fill in the blanks.

Reminders:
There are no right or wrong answers.
Handwriting and spelling don't count.
All answers are confidential.

When you know facts, you do not have to guess why something happened or what took place. Distinguish facts from rumors, wishes, half-truths, guesses, or prejudicial remarks.

Facts convey the truth. Facts can be easy or hard to accept. We need a lot of facts in order to understand complicated situations. Sometimes we cannot get facts and this can be upsetting—like *why* did that grownup hurt that child?

Facts about yourself promote self-understanding. "I can do well in math." "I am a giving person." "I need help in science." "I am a good friend."

Make a list of some of the **facts** you know about you. (height, weight, talents, favorite books, music, etc.)

_____

_____

_____

Make a list of **facts** about your best friend.

_____

_____

Children are often interested in their family history. What **facts** would you like to know about *your* family background? Empower yourself to ask.

_____

_____

_____

Some **facts** are sad. Do you think children should be told sad facts—such as "Grandfather is very ill?" Explain your answer.

_____

_____

_____

_____

There are reasons why someone tells you, "You are too young to understand." The person may think you either cannot accept the **facts** or that it is something you should not be told. Sometimes a person does not want you to be upset or is afraid *he or she* may not be able to cope with your being upset. What do you think about these ideas?

_____

_____

_____

Kids hate to be lied to. If someone is not telling you the truth, how can you ask them to tell you **facts?** What words would you choose?

_____

_____

_____

There are some **facts** that help kids understand family problems. For example, the decision to get a divorce is a grownup decision. A child is not to blame. Another example is that kids cannot stop a parent from drinking too much, and people who are violent can get help: Clinics, doctors, and special groups are available. Are there some **facts** you would like to know about a family problem?

_____

_____

_____

_____

Kids feel unimportant when their parents do not explain what happened in the family before they were born—or when they were little. They want **facts.** Do you agree with this statement?

_____

_____

_____

When a child has trouble learning in school, it is important to understand why. Teachers should give kids **facts** about their problems and explain learning disabilities—including how stress can affect memory. With explanations—the **facts** about learning—a child will be less discouraged.
Do you have any problems that you would like to have explained?

_____

_____

_____

_____

_____

Ask people to tell you facts. When someone tells you facts, they are showing respect. You feel good when others show you respect.

details from his tests, academic work, and relevant professional books or resources. A child can understand disabilities and be encouraged to use help. The more a child understands, the easier it is to accept and remediate learning difficulties and maintain a positive self-concept.

Promote Discussion

Select items from Activity 4–1.

End of the Session

Set the time for the next one-to-one session.

End with an optimistic personal statement such as, "I'm looking forward to seeing you again. I'm sure we can. . . ."

Use affirmations. Repeat instructions as often as necessary.

> **Healing is taking place when children display that they can handle difficult facts with increased competency. Assimilating difficult facts may be painful. It is a struggle. It is a necessity for Children Who Hurt.**

SHELLY AND MISS TIPTON TALK ABOUT FACTS

Shelly is morose. She isn't hostile to other children. She does what Miss Tipton asks her to do. Her work is complete. She acts sad and spacy.

When she and Miss Tipton are alone together, Miss Tipton follows the customary Trust Building Program pattern. She starts with a positive comment. "I'm really pleased that you are showing more interest in reading, Shelly. Keep up the good work."

Miss Tipton reads the little girl her comments from the Struggles Chart that she has filled out.

Shelly smiled at Mary today. Seems more withdrawn than usual.

Shelly had a happy few moments today. Chose to share in Our Facts and Feelings Forum—a first for Shelly. It was the first time she talked about herself.

Shelly told the class, "My facts today are that my mother and daddy were divorced when I was a baby. My mother was only seventeen years old when I was born. I live with my dad and grandmother. Sometimes I wish my mom and dad would be together again. Three different women call my dad on the phone. He says he is never going to get married again."

"Shelly, I can see that you are trying to be more friendly. I am proud of you. I also notice when you seem sad."

Miss Tipton selects some sentences from the Activities Pages which she reads to Shelly. *Kids feel unimportant when their parents do not explain what happened in the family before they were born or when they were little. They want the **facts**. Do you agree with this statement?*

Shelly starts to cry. "I'll tell you, Miss Tipton, what *I* would like to know. Why did my mom leave us? Why didn't my dad make her stay with us? Why doesn't she come back now? She and Dad talk on the phone once in a while and I never hear them fight. Why does my grandmother say mean things about my mom and then act so nice to me and my dad? Isn't a grandmother supposed to say nice things about everybody?"

After a pause, she continues. "Why can't I live with my mom? I really want to know."

Miss Tipton takes hold of Shelly's hand and holds it for a short while. "I'm sorry that I can't answer your questions," she says quietly. She decides to talk about teenage marriages. She hopes this will help.

She explains that many teen marriages break up because one or both parents cannot manage to be a wife or husband and a parent and a high-school student at the same time. The mother and dad can remain friends even though one parent leaves. The absent parent may love the child and still not see her very often. She says that custody arrangements are made by a judge.

Shelly picks up her pencil. "Mom was seventeen when I was born. I am almost seven. That means she is twenty-four now. She's old enough to come back."

"It's a lot more complicated than that," her teacher explains. "Shelly, I cannot answer your questions about your parents. Why don't you ask your grandmother or dad what you want to know? You're a bright girl. You can understand many things. You are *entitled* to know what happened."

"I've been thinking about it a lot. I'm afraid Dad or Grandma would get mad. It's like what happened is a *big secret*. It's hard to live in a house with secrets."

Miss Tipton says she will try to find a book about divorce for Shelly to take home for her grandma or dad to read; maybe that will open up a conversation. Maybe then Shelly can ask for the facts about what happened.

Shelly isn't satisfied. "Why can't you ask my grandmother or my father for me? My grandma tells my aunt all kinds of things—like how to make apricot jam and where to buy boots. Those are facts. Why wouldn't she tell you facts about when I was little?"

"Teachers do not usually inquire about such matters. I'm concerned about *you*, Shelly, and how you are getting along in school. I want to be someone you trust. I am not keeping any secrets from you. I encourage you to ask your dad or grandmother what you want to know." After some further discussion, she hands Shelly a book called *Babies Having Babies*. "Ask your grandmother to read this book to you. You'll find it interesting."

They end the session with affirmations. "I deserve to know the facts about what happened when I was little." "I deserve to hear, 'You are old enough to understand about when teenagers get married.' "

"That sounds good," she adds as she leaves.

The next day, Shelly is angry. "No one read me that book. Dad wasn't home and Grandma was talking on the phone. She told me to put the book on the kitchen table and she'd look at it later.

"When I went to bed, my grandmother said she didn't have time to read the book tonight. Maybe tomorrow. She said it didn't look very interesting. She also said, 'I hope you are happy with me, Shelly. I love you, you know.' Maybe she needs to see that page you read me about 'kids need facts to help them cope.' It's a fancy sentence but I understand it."

Miss Tipton reassures Shelly, "You are lovable, indeed."

ROGER AND MRS. SNYDER TALK ABOUT FACTS

"Last night, my dad hit my mom," Roger tells Mrs. Snyder as they start a one-to-one session. He doesn't sound upset. He talks about it as if saying, "It is raining outside."

Mrs. Snyder is concerned. Most kids don't make announcements like this. She decides to follow the Trust Building Program session pattern rather than ask for details. In a few minutes, she will ask Roger about his feelings and concerns.

"I'm sure that this must be upsetting to you, Roger," she begins. "I want to compliment you on that interesting report you wrote on racing cars. And I noticed that you and Fred were playing a video game together and seemed to be having a good time." She looks at the Struggles Chart she has filled in. "Oh, I forgot to mention that I was glad to see you volunteer as a school guide when the foreign visitors came."

Roger speaks up, "Fred called me on the phone—just to talk. I forgot to get his number. I'll ask him for it today. I like him."

Mrs. Snyder introduces the Activities Pages about facts. Roger reads them over quickly and selects two items.

"Many parents have problems that they do not discuss with the children. What do you think of that?"

"There are some **facts** that help kids understand family problems. For example, the decision to get a divorce is a grownup decision. A child is not to blame. Kids cannot stop a parent from drinking too much. People who are violent can get help. Are there some **facts** you would like to know about a family problem?"

Roger says, "I want to talk about what happened last night and my dad's drinking first. We've never talked about it before. My dad drinks too much. Why does he drink? Will he always be a drunk?"

Mrs. Snyder is businesslike. "Many people who drink *cannot* control how much they drink or how they behave when they drink too much. They can get help."

"But suppose he doesn't want to, then what?"

"Well, Roger, no one can make him quit, but *you* can take care of you when he is upset. Do your best to stay out of his way, don't argue, and afterwards, don't pay any attention to his excuses. That may help."

She picks up a small article that she has cut out of the newspaper. She reads it out loud.

"In more than half of the homes where there is violence, one or more persons has a drinking problem. One-half of all automobile accidents involve alcohol. In the United States, 100,000 elementary school children get drunk at least once a week. Most teenage drinkers started drinking in the fourth or fifth grade. It's a serious problem, Roger."

Roger says that he knows two kids in the sixth grade who live in his neighborhood who drink a lot of beer. "I hear them laughing a lot and one kid says he wants to quit school but he's too young."

Roger mentions his dad again. "When I talk to Mom about Dad drinking so much, she says, 'All men get drunk, Roger. That's how they relax.' It's like she doesn't want to believe that my dad is different."

"You're a wise young man, Roger. You really figured that out. We both know that *all* men don't get drunk. Maybe you could start to collect newspaper articles about drinking and accidents and all those *facts*. That might be a way to start talking about the problem, and meanwhile, you could tell your dad that you are worried. I'm here to give *you* support."

"Tell me about people who hurt other people," Roger says.

Mrs. Snyder says, "Everyone gets angry once in a while but most people do not show their anger by hurting someone or something. People who hurt others usually have a lot of problems. They may be lonely or drink too much or have a lot of worries or stress. People can learn to express anger without hurting others, but they may not be able to control their aggression when they've had too much to drink. That's why it's important for you and your mom to stay out of the way and not argue with your dad when he is drunk."

"What can *I* do to help my dad?" Roger asks.

"You know that I have a "time-out" place where I send kids who are angry or upset. You could talk to your dad about time-outs. I know grownups can use time-outs, too. Some people learn to count to ten or take three deep breaths and that helps. Others may go for a walk or a run.

"It makes me sad and mad," Roger adds. "Thanks for talking to me about drinking. It's a lot to think about."

Roger and Mrs. Snyder agree that they will meet two days later.

He remembers to make up an affirmation as he walks out the door.

"I deserve to know the facts about drinking and to learn about people who get violent. I deserve to have people tell me, 'It's not your fault that your dad drinks too much.' "

TIM AND MR. ATKINS TALK ABOUT FACTS

Tim tells Mr. Atkins he is confused and wants to know what is going on. He took a note home to his mother to ask for her permission to have him tested. "Does that mean I'm dumb? Does that mean I can't come to this school anymore?"

"Calm down, Tim. You've been tested before and you know nothing drastic is going to happen. Let's talk about learning disabilities—in this school that's the name they use for your learning problems. You can be very smart and still have problems. We try to help any kid who has poor study habits, who is two grade levels behind in reading and says that he is 'no good.' That sounds like you, doesn't it?"

Tim isn't impressed. "Isn't it about time somebody explained all this stuff to me? Mr. Atkins—tell me the *facts*—what am I supposed to learn when I go with that aide? I'd rather stay in class. Besides, Mr. Atkins, why have special help with all those books and machines when I still have to use regular sixth grade books in all my other classes?"

"Those are tough questions, Tim. They are one reason you get discouraged."

Mr. Atkins and Tim read the question on the Activities Pages about when a child has trouble learning in school.

"When a child has trouble learning in school, it is important to understand why. Teachers should give kids **facts** about their problems and explain learning disabilities including how stress can affect memory. With explanations—the **facts** about learning—the child will be less discouraged. . . . Do you have any problems that you would like to have explained?"

Mr. Atkins says, "Tim, most kids don't choose that question. I'm glad you did."

Here are some problems that a sixth grader may have.

Handwriting is difficult to read.	Gets distracted easily.
Feels discouraged a lot.	Is disorganized.
Is moody.	Has poor study habits.
Is angry a lot.	Tends to have trouble making friends.
May use drugs or alcohol as an escape.	Gets depressed.

Can't remember what he reads.

Has a physical problem with vision or hearing.

Unable to take teasing, jokes.

Can't remember what he hears.

Mr. Atkins explains, "A child can have a learning problem in one area—such as in seeing accurately—and be fine in others. Kids who are upset find it hard to memorize. Others cannot recognize sounds or have trouble speaking. In order to get help in special classes, they have to be tested. You understand that, don't you?"

Tim looks glum. "A lot of those things sound like me. At least I don't do drugs," he says.

"Good boy, Tim. And you can get help with your reading in the resource room. It seems as if your eyes are the problem. Let me tell you some facts about kids who didn't get help for their learning problems. Ninety percent of the kids who go to detention centers or get in trouble with the law have had learning problems that were *not* discovered, or they didn't get enough help or the right kind of help. They got very discouraged. A lot of them quit school and then stole cars or got busted for dealing drugs or something else.

"I've had some kind of help every year, Mr. A. Why doesn't it do any good?"

"It does, Tim. You are doing much better in spelling. This testing is so they can keep you in some special classes and give you extra time on the computers."

Tim changes the subject. "I also want some facts about what happened when my dad died. There seems to be a family secret and I'm tired of it. You know, even if he did do something wrong, I have a right to know. I'm old enough to understand a lot about people. I'll do some looking around the house for old letters or pictures and then we can talk. I'm glad you understand that a guy needs to know about his dad."

Mr. Atkins takes this seriously. He tells the boy, "I had a rough time as a kid. There weren't many Black families in our neighborhood and the kids used to tease me. I used to pretend it didn't bother me, but it did. My mother was a nurse and my dad was a cop. He got killed when I was ten. We stayed in the neighborhood because of some insurance. I was jealous of the white kids and especially jealous of kids who had a dad. It's not easy to be a fatherless boy. I had nothing to be ashamed of but that took me a long time to learn. When I applied to go to college to learn to be a teacher, I thought they wouldn't let me in because I didn't have a dad. I really believed that. I was wrong. Maybe you've got some thoughts like that that we can talk about. We don't have to have the facts about what happened to your dad in order to talk about you.

"I'll see you on Thursday at the same time. Meanwhile, Tim, hang in there. Your eyes may play tricks on you but you are a good kid. How about a high five and an affirmation?"

Their hands clap together. Tim says, "I deserve to be told about learning problems. Maybe some day I'll get the picture that you can be smart and still have problems."

He is in no hurry to leave Mr. Atkins' office. He hangs around until the bell rings. Then he says, "Guess I better go," as he walks slowly out of the gym on the way to his next class.

MARY AND MRS. BRYCE TALK ABOUT FACTS

Mary walks up behind Paul while he is bent over his locker trying to take out a book. With her knees, she pushes him. He falls into the locker. Mary laughs and her friends do, too. It makes Paul angry.

"Hey, chick, keep your knees to yourself. What are you looking for anyway? You want someone to push you around?" He doesn't wait for an answer. He walks off.

The girls say Paul is rude. Mary says, "I think he's kinda cute. He's got a nice butt—I'll push him again. Maybe next time he'll like it."

Barb asks, "Suppose he hits you? Suppose he grabs your hair? You may be asking for trouble."

Mrs. Bryce overhears the conversation. Mary pretends she doesn't see her when she walks by. When they meet for a Confidence Building Session, Mrs. Bryce commends her for coming to school on time every day this week. Mary is honest: "I like it better at school than I do at home."

Mary adds, dejectedly, "I suppose you want to talk about what happened in the hall. I didn't hurt the guy."

"Mary, I'm on a committee with some people from the high school. We are developing an "Up With Kids" program for students who are turned off to school. A lot of the girls spend most of their time worrying about their looks, making wise remarks, and chasing boys."

"What's that got to do with me?" Mary wants to know.

"I'm concerned about your attitude—and I don't want you heading in the wrong direction. Let's talk straight. The fact is—girls with those problems usually do not like themselves. They have a poor self-concept. They lack self-esteem. A lot of them get into trouble with the boys."

"What is this, Mrs. Bryce—some kind of a lecture? I'm leaving," she says as she stands up.

"Hold it, Mary. I'm talking about why kids do what they do and I don't want you getting hurt if you tease some boy and he hauls off and hits you. Sit down."

"I'm no drop-out, Mrs. Bryce. I'm no different from most of the kids around here. So I like to tease boys. So what?"

"Mary, pushing boys with your knees can be a come-on. A lot of the ninth graders are big and tough. Some of them can get violent—especially if they are in a bad mood—and they can be moody. Some are on drugs. Some are pretty experienced with girls. You might get hurt, and I don't want that to happen to you."

"Stop worrying. I can take care of myself."

Mary looks crusty. She is anxious to get out of the counselor's office and join her girlfriends.

Mrs. Bryce asks, "Is there something new bothering you?"

"I want to run away from home."

"Are you serious, Mary?"

"My mom criticizes everything I do. She can't stand what I wear, how I fix my hair, or who I talk to on the phone. I've had it."

Mrs. Bryce doesn't hesitate to take charge of the Confidence Building Session. She tells Mary, "Sometimes kids feel that they are more grown up than their parents. And maybe, in some ways, they understand other kids better. But when things are unpleasant at home, everybody gets uptight. When moms get critical, it's mostly because they care."

Mary listens. "Not in my house, Mrs. Bryce. You don't understand. My mom couldn't care less. I've been thinking about leaving for a long time. I am a nobody at my house. Jenny said she'd go with me, and I've got $45.82 to get a bus ticket. My cousin ran away two years ago. She came back at Christmas and told me she had a great time."

"How old is she?"

"Seventeen, I think."

"There's a big difference between seventeen and thirteen, Mary. You know that. How would you support yourself and what about school? I will tell you what I believe. *If you run away, you are not taking care of yourself. If you need to be away from home for a short while, we can talk about that.*"

Mary's expression changes. "I guess I just needed to tell you how unhappy I am. I won't split—but I'd like to."

The rest of their time together they talk about runaways. Mrs. Bryce hands her a paper called *Facts About Kids Who Run Away.* "I thought this might be of interest." Mary puts it in her notebook. "You know, I deserve some decent attention from my family."

That night she reads the paper Mrs. Bryce has given her.

Facts About Kids Who Run Away *Each year about one million teenagers run away from home. They are divided into two groups. One is the group who runs away or is thrown out of the home. Most of these kids are depressed, angry, troubled, or seeking help. Many have been on drugs. Many have been abused either physically, sexually, or emotionally. They feel that they have no one at home who cares about them. They usually end up lonely, in trouble with the law, quitting school, or attempting suicide.*

The second group consists of kids who are assertive and committed to a new way of living. Some have adults they can depend on to help them. Some have a definite place to go and feel that they would benefit by being away from a dysfunctional family. Most runaways are in the first group.

Being away from home may give kids a chance to redefine their relationships with parents. Most kids who run away are at least fourteen or fifteen years old. Very few girls are under fourteen years of age.

Most runaways spend their time just "hanging around." Most are forced to become street people or prostitutes to get money. Few jobs are available to transients.

Runaways lose interest in school and family. They become close to other runaways or new people that they meet. Few runaways like what they are doing and how they live. Some are never seen again. Living on the street can be miserable—the loss of family ties is a great sadness. Many report they regret leaving home.

Mary mumbles to herself as she gets into bed, "I guess a lot of kids think about running away when things don't go right. It sounds kinda grim. I'll just talk to Mrs. Bryce. She understands kids." She turns on her boom box, tunes in her favorite station, and turns off the light.

STEP FIVE
CHOICES/OPTIONS—STOP! THINK! AND CHOOSE!—ONE WAY TO MANAGE BEHAVIOR

Background

The world of decision making is a difficult one for Children Who Hurt. Like frightened animals, they learn to freeze, hide, or attack. The purpose of this step of the Trust Building Program is to help frightened children *decide* or *choose* what to say or how to act. It is to help children learn to manage their behavior so that they feel self-assured. It introduces them to options. It helps them *examine and eliminate self-defeating habits and to acquire a positive outlook.* This is a tremendous task.

Children Who Hurt must, of necessity, make many decisions which are reality- or survival-oriented.

"Gotta get along with my stepdad" or "gotta fix my own lunch—mom has a hangover" are sensitive decisions some children must make.

Children cannot visualize or choose positive responses when paralyzed with fear or depression. They have to be in a relationship with you that is not frightening in order to learn to *Stop! Think! and Choose!* In the one-to-one sessions, they have to be taught to think of options and choose positive ways to interact with people.

These stories may help you to become acquainted with the Stop! Think! and Choose! method.

Sample Story Number One Mary's friend, Rachel, wouldn't sit next to her on the bus. Mary says, "Okay, *stupid*, have it your way. And I won't have lunch with you today." The friend snaps, "Then forget about going skating on Saturday."

They both feel bad.

What else could Mary have said or asked? Mary could have asked, "Rachel, how come you won't sit next to me?"

Possible answer: "I want to read my social studies."

Mary could have asked, "Rachel, do you just feel like being alone?"

Possible answer: "Yeah, I didn't sleep much last night and I'm tired. See you at lunch."

Mary could have asked, "Rachel, do you want to sit by yourself because you're thinking about what happened when you lost your notebook?"

Possible answer: "Yeah, I was wondering how I could make up my work."

But instead, Mary chooses to call her stupid. Mary takes it personally when Rachel wants to be alone. Mary could have asked other questions which might have prevented the misunderstanding and the bad feelings. *Mary did not stop to think of her options.*

Sample Story Number Two   Greg is between classes talking to his friend in the hall. Suddenly, Jim walks by, grabs Greg's notebook, throws it on the floor, and walks off.

Greg picks up the notebook and decides to catch up with Jim and smash the book across his back. Jim grabs it again and yells, "What's your problem? Can't you take a joke?" A teacher sees Greg hit Jim. Hitting is not allowed. Greg gets into trouble.

What else could Greg have done?

- He could have picked up the notebook and said to himself, "Something must be bugging Jim."

- He could wait till an appropriate time to tell Jim to quit being a jerk.

- He could acknowledge to himself that he "hates" Jim right now.

- He could have come to you and talked about what's going on.

- He could have ignored it. He knows Jim is a bully; he teases lots of kids.

- He could have laughed at Jim and explained to himself, "He just wants my attention. He's an okay kid but that's not much of an approach."

Any of these *choices* would have prevented Greg from getting into trouble.

Sample Story Number Three   Focus is on a "pretend" home situation. A mom and dad are arguing at the table. The dad calls the mom a dirty name. Without thinking, the boy tells his dad to shut up. The dad turns to the boy and tells him to mind his own business. But the boy is part of this family—part of this scene. He feels frustrated and frightened.

The boy yells, "Dad, sometimes I wish you'd get out of here."

The boy leaves the table. He would like to cry.

Did it do any good to talk to the dad like that? *No!* It could have made things much worse. No matter what the boy said, it probably wouldn't have stopped the fighting. It was not his fight. *A child is not responsible for how parents act.*

What else could he have done?		*What else could he have said?*
Leave the table	Read to his sister or brother	He could have said, "I can't stand this. I'm going to leave," or he could have said nothing.
Go do the dishes	Call a friend on the phone	
Start his homework	Take a shower or bath	
Watch TV		

Stop! Think! and Choose! empowers Children Who Hurt to begin to believe no one decides for you what you will say or do. You choose to smile or frown. You choose your words. You are in charge of you.

Stop! Think! and Choose! is a tool to use so that a person feels in control. One can get in the habit of making positive choices. One can learn to stop saying and doing unfriendly things—even if upset or afraid. One can click into the habit of asking instantly, "What else can I say or do?" or *"What options do I have?"* Little people pick up quickly on phrases such as, "That's not a nice thing to do. I better not do it." or "Mom might like that. I'll do it." Older children are equally adept at acquiring the method. *But they must be taught and encouraged, and one-to-one sessions with you provide such opportunities.* Their time with you may be the only time they are pain-free and willing to imagine happy endings or good things. When they are with someone they trust—once they trust—they can begin to become aware or accept that they can choose what they say and do.

Stop! Think! and Choose! helps check impulsiveness. An immature Child Who Hurts is prone to be unduly impulsive. When the habit of Stop! Think! and Choose! is acquired, the child will use it everywhere—even at home when things are in chaos. This is a triumph!

Reminders for Adults You may smile as you recall your grandmother's familiar warning "Think before you speak." Now, you hear yourself adapting this phrase into a dynamic model of Stop! Think! and Choose! Appreciate the fact that you, too, may be revered just like your "Grammie."

Strategies for One-to-One Sessions

Purpose: To teach children to manage their behavior by using the method of *Stop* before you act, *Think* of your options and *Choose* what you do or say so that you will not be sorry later. To encourage children to ask themselves routinely, "What else can I say or do?"

To help children understand that they can control what they say and do and choose positive, friendly behavior instead of negative or self-defeating behaviors. To help children begin to break old habits and change old attitudes.

Directions: Explain and practice *Stop! Think! and Choose! A Way to Manage Behavior.* Use your own vocabulary. Create numerous examples.

Important Teacher Statements to Express to a Student People often do or say things that they regret. They need to learn how to Stop! Think! and Choose! They will *stop* before they act and *think* of answers to these two questions:

"What different things can I do," or "What different things can I say?"

Then they *choose* to do or say something which is friendly, positive, or helpful. They will feel more self-confident when they get in the habit of not saying or doing things that they will regret.

I will help you practice this method. Soon you will say, "I did it. I said the right things," or "I didn't do it and I'm glad of that." Then you will know that *you are in charge of you—that you can manage your behavior.* These are difficult lessons for girls and boys to learn. I'm sure you can do it.

Show the student this box

Learn to ask:
    What else can I do or say now?
Learn to say:
    I get to choose. I get to decide.
Practice thinking:
    I can be friendly, positive and helpful.

Have the child repeat the following sentences to understand and demonstrate choices If I say something friendly, I *choose* to be friendly.

If I do something nasty, I *choose* to do something nasty.

Have the child make up similar statements

Most smiles are started by another smile.

Help the child learn to distinguish between positive and negative messages—both verbal and nonverbal Mention that the child will be happier when in the habit of giving positive messages.

Positive Statements One Can Choose:

- *Thank yous*: "Thanks for lending me the book."

- *Compliment*: "Good job." "I'm glad you're my friend."

- *Encouragement*: "You can do it." "Go for it." "Try again."

- *Optimistic Outlook*: "We'll get the job done." "I'll make the team." "Things will get better." "We'll figure out a way to clean up this mess."

Negative Statements One Can Choose:

- *Refusal to respond—unenthusiastic when praised*: "It was no big deal." "You may think it's great, but it's not great for me." "Don't bug me. I don't want to talk."

- *Put-downs, name-calling*: "Any jerk could have done that." "Why don't you get your act together?" "You're stupid."

- *Discouragement*: "It won't work." "Why try?" "Nobody ever gives me a break." "She'll never like me."

- *Negative outlook*: "I'll never be lucky. He'll never stop pushing me around." "I'm dumb now and I'll always be dumb."

Note: When you verbalize positive thoughts and happy endings, they may be ridiculed by the Child Who Hurts. Thinking happy thoughts or dreaming happy dreams may be difficult, if not impossible, for this child. It is too painful for the child to imagine happy things while living in an unhappy situation. He or she may be accustomed to insults or neglect. It is a way of life for many.

Help the child become aware of personal attitudes and habits Ask the student, "Do you think *you* are bossy, friendly, grouchy, mean, nice or silly (or whatever)?"

Emphasize nonverbal messages. As examples, a person *chooses* to smile, frown, hit, hide, stiffen up, or be affectionate.

Have the child complete the following exercises to illustrate how one's behavior may affect others

When I said (or did) what I did,

I was being . . .	*The other person . . .*

__friendly (cite example)	smiled, called on the phone
__nasty (cite example)	walked away
__impatient (cite example)	started to cry
__unselfish	_____
__helpful	_____
__funny	_____
__sarcastic	_____

No one makes your decisions for you

Explain Response   After you say or do something, how another person reacts or feels is called a *response*.

Think about what the other person may do or how she may feel if you say or do something

Will the person get mad?	Will the person feel happy?
Will the person smile?	Will the person feel helpless?
Will the person walk away?	Will the person feel proud?

Take care of yourself and your relationships by using your judgment, common sense, and self-control. Remember to Stop! Think! and Choose!

Promote Discussion

Read statements from Activity 5–1. Encourage the child to express feelings and ask questions.

End of the Session

Set the time for the next one-to-one session.
End with an optimistic, personal statement: "I'm looking forward to seeing you. I'm sure we can. . . ."
Use affirmations. Repeat instructions as often as necessary.

OPTIONS/CHOICES
STOP! THINK! AND CHOOSE! ONE WAY TO MANAGE BEHAVIOR

Directions: Read the information and fill in the blanks.

Reminders:
There are no right or wrong answers.
Handwriting and spelling don't count.
All answers are confidential.

In almost every situation, you can stop and ask yourself, "**What things can I say or do right now?**" and "**Which one should I choose?**" You can do this even when you are mad, scared or sad. Filling in this page will help you think about **choices**.
Your answers may be discussed in your one-to-one sessions.

Sample Story
Jimmy is mad at Harry. He wants to hit him. He stops. He asks himself, "What else can I do?" He chooses to walk away. He could call Harry a dirty name or write, "Harry is dumb" on the board or tell his sister, "I *hate* Harry." He controls his hands. He does not hit. He is glad he chooses to walk away.

Make up several endings for the following.
Harry is hiding Jim's hat, and Jim is tired of being teased. Instead of throwing a snowball at Harry, Jimmy decides to . . .

_____

_____

_____

_____

Sally asks the same question over and over. Janie gets annoyed. Instead of hurting Sally's feelings by calling her stupid or dumb, Janie chooses to . . .

_____

_____

_____

_____

_____

Instead of laughing at Sally when she falls down, Janie chooses to . . .

_____

_____

_____

_____

Activity 5-1, continued

_____

_____

Harry is talking loudly while Jim is trying to read. Instead of yelling at Harry to shut
up, Jimmy chooses to . . .

_____

_____

_____

_____

It is especially hard to Stop! Think! and Choose! when you are angry.
Things to remember about anger:
Everyone gets angry.
Sometimes people act angry when they are really sad or afraid.
Even when a person is angry, that does not mean that he or she has the right to hurt
others.
Make a list of five ways of showing anger besides hurting someone.

_____

_____

_____

_____

_____

How do you feel about name-calling and put-downs?

_____

_____

You can say _thank you_ or tell others that you like what they do, how they help you
or what they give to you.
For example, Fred's teacher explains a problem to him three times. She is very pa
tient. Fred says, "Thank you. I appreciate your help." He can also say:
"I feel better when I know what to do." or
"That was neat that you took time to help me."
Even nice expressions take practice.
Ginny has been sick. Many classmates sent her cards. When she comes back to
school, she says . . .

_____

_____

_____

A box of pencils slips out of Dick's hands and pencils scatter over the floor. Bill helps Dick pick them up. Dick says . . .

_____

_____

_____

The class goes on an interesting field trip. When everyone returns to school, Jenny tells the teacher . . .

_____

_____

_____

_____

How do you feel when you do something for someone and he or she doesn't say something nice?

_____

_____

_____

_____

_____

Why is it easier for some kids to say mean things rather than nice things?

_____

_____

_____

How would you help someone to choose nice things to say?

_____

_____

_____

_____

> **Making hurtful or unkind choices or decisions is not a good habit. Good choices help you feel good about you.**

> The ultimate criterion for personal growth is the extent to which positive behavior derives from self-control rather than external control.*
>
> **Fagen, Long, and Stevens**

MISS TIPTON INTRODUCES SHELLY TO STOP! THINK! AND CHOOSE!

"Why can't you make those kids play with me? Yesterday I let Mary have the yellow marker and she only had to ask for it once. But when the kids went out at recess, nobody even talked to me. They don't act friendly at all. In fact, they were mean, called me a baby and said they were going to bring me a diaper."

"What did you do?"

"I stuck out my tongue. I said, 'I hate you.' One of the kids said, 'Stop acting like a monster, Shelly.' That's when I decided to tell you how mean they are."

"Shelly, you're not a monster. Maybe this book will give you some ideas on how you can work things out with the girls. I know that everyone wants a best friend or other kids to play with." She picks up *Have You Hugged a Monster Today.*** She reads, *Sometimes the people around us seem like monsters, but have you ever thought how tough it must be to be a monster? It's not an easy job. Being out of the 'in' crowd can get to be kind of lonely sometimes. Monsters are really nice people who sometimes lose control of themselves—gentle creatures who are soft inside but who think they have to act tough on the outside. That's all monsters are. Now you don't have to be so afraid of monsters, do you?*

Shelly interrupts, "I am *not* a monster, Miss Tipton. I don't care what that book says."

"Shelly, I wasn't talking about you. Let's read more of the book and see how it can be helpful," she remarks.

Most monsters have had it a little rough in life. They started out as very nice people but then something happened to them. Being a monster is no easy job. Monsters need love, too. Maybe even a little more than you and me. So the next time you run into a monster, give him a hug.

Oh, yes—one more thing. Do you ever feel like a monster? It's not unusual, you know. Not all of us are angels all the time. Sometimes even the best of people make the silliest mistakes. So the next time you feel like a monster, give yourself a hug—send yourself some love. You really are pretty beautiful, you know.

---

* Stanley A. Fagen, Nicholas J. Long, and Donald J. Stevens, *Teaching Children Self-Control,* Columbus, Ohio: Charles E. Merrill, 1975.

**Alan Cohen, *Have You Hugged a Monster Today,* Haiku, Hawaii 96708: Alan Cohen Publications, 1982.

Shelly wants to know, "Why should I be nice to them when they are not nice to me? And I am *not* a monster and I'm not going to hug them."

Miss Tipton is disappointed that Shelly is still defensive. "Shelly, I think a few smiles might be a good beginning. What ideas do you have for how to make friends or how you could act more friendly?"

No answer.

Miss Tipton continues, "I want you to decide to be friendly and do friendly things. You can smile at the girls, you can stop saying, 'I hate you,' you can bring something to share, you can tell them about you—your favorite food, colors, your dog, or fun things you do with your grandmother or your dad. You can pretend that you don't hear them when they say things that you don't like. You can offer to help when they are making a project."

Shelly answers, "I suppose so." Then tears come to her eyes. She tells Miss Tipton, "It really hurt my feelings when Jenny handed out the invitations to her birthday party and I didn't get one. Why didn't her mother mail them to the kids so I didn't have to know about it?"

"I'm not sure why Jenny brought them to school, Shelly. I'm afraid a lot of kids had their feelings hurt. You're not the only one." Then she smiled as she says, "I wasn't invited either. Teachers don't get asked to parties very often."

Shelly reassures her, "If I ever have a party, you can come!"

"Thanks, Shelly. But let's talk some more about the different ways you can change how you act around the other kids so you will be a happier girl." They talk about Stop! Think! and Choose! and Miss Tipton reads her stories from the Activities Pages. At first Shelly backs off. "That sounds too grownup for me." Miss Tipton persuades her to try. Shelly is animated when she says, "Hey, I get it. Mean kids choose mean things to say and friendly kids choose friendly things."

Towards the end of the one-to-one session, her teacher agrees to lend her the Monster book so that her grandmother can read the rest of it to her. Shelly mumbles as she leaves, "*Stop* doing things that are unfriendly. *Think* of different ways to be friendly, and *Choose* one and do it, *and I deserve a friend* because I don't hit and now I share markers."

MRS. SNYDER INTRODUCES ROGER TO STOP! THINK! AND CHOOSE!

Roger throws a snowball at Charlie and hits him in the face. The teacher at the bus escorts him in to see the principal. Mrs. Snyder is called to the office. Without hesitating, the principal and Mrs. Snyder enforce the school rules—snowball throwing is punished by no recess for five days, and indoor recess only for five days after that. They lecture him about the danger involved. Roger mutters, "Ten days is a long time," as he walks back to class.

That afternoon, Roger and Mrs. Snyder meet at their usual time. Roger is picking away at the zipper on his boots when his teacher steps into the room. She smiles softly and says, "I am glad we have this time together, Roger. I need to understand what happened this morning."

Roger expects Mrs. Snyder to be angry or to begin their session by saying that she is disappointed in him. He even flashes on the idea that she might announce that their Trust Building Program is finished. He shakes his head from side to side. He waits for her to go on.

"Roger, I know that it takes weeks and weeks to learn to trust. It also takes weeks to learn new ways to show that you are angry. I am sorry that something upset you this morning and that you lost control. You are still special to me. Please tell me what happened on the bus."

"Charlie called my mother a dirty name. He's done it lots of times before. Today it really made me mad. I lost my cool."

"What else could you have done?"

"I dunno."

Mrs. Snyder knows Roger is not a liar. She says, "Roger, we need to work on *Stop! Think! and Choose!* It will help you think of choices and to manage what you do and say." She slowly explains the method, and then selects several stories from the Activities Pages. She repeats the question, "What else could the person have said or done?" over and over again. Roger makes up new endings for the stories.

Roger complains, "I can think of things to do when I'm in here, but it's not so easy when I'm *really* mad. Besides, he deserved it. Why should he get away with calling my mother a bad name?"

"I can't defend Charlie, Roger, but I can try to help you make choices that help you feel good about *you*. Let's look at it. He acts like a jerk and you end up in trouble. Is it worth it?"

Roger's answer is simple: "Recess is no big deal. I still think he has no right to talk about my mom like that."

"I'll ask again, Roger. *What else could you have done? What else could you have said?*"

"Well, I could have done things like that kid in the story—called him a name or thrown a snowball at a tree and all that stuff, But how do you learn to stop when you're mad? My dad does whatever he wants to when he's mad."

"Flash on it. Flash on the word *'Stop.'* And ask, 'Will I be sorry if I say that?' Look out for you. Let's pretend that you're mad at me. What would you do?"

"C'mon—you're a grownup and besides, I like you. I hate Charlie."

"*The person you have to like is you* and you've got to choose what's best for you. If Charlie has a big mouth, that's his problem—not yours."

"It's my problem when he talks about my mom."

"Your reaction is your problem, Roger. What else could you have done?"

Roger says slowly, "I really don't know."

Mrs. Snyder makes up more stories with characters who are mad, sad, or scared. Some are out of control, some say mean things and others just make faces. She tells about when she was little and called her mother a witch. She wasn't really sorry until that night when her dad came home and washed her mouth out with soap. That's when she started to keep a journal where she could write anything she wanted to and not get in trouble. Finally Roger says, "I get it. If you're the one who would get into trouble, *don't* do it. And if you do something nice and the other person acts more friendly, *do it.*"

Then he complains, "At my house, nobody does anything nice for me."

His teacher suggests, "Why not start a new routine and see if it works. Tell your mom tonight, 'That was a great dinner, Mom. Thanks.' See what happens. Even if she doesn't say anything, you chose to be friendly—even to your mom—and that's practice, Roger. It sounds old-fashioned, Rog, but practice does make perfect and you have to start somewhere. Do it. You'll be glad that you did."

"I dunno," Roger says as he gets up to leave. "I almost forgot about those nice things about me that I'm supposed to say. So here goes. "I'm an 'okay kid' and I can learn to be careful about what I say. But I still think Charlie is a nerd." Roger makes a funny face as he leaves.

MR. ATKINS INTRODUCES TIM
TO STOP! THINK! AND CHOOSE!

"I gotta tell you something, Mr. Atkins. I said something nice to a kid today just because you've been nagging me to be more friendly. The kid looked at me as if I was nuts. He said, 'What do you want—some money?' It was weird. I couldn't figure out what to do."

"So he didn't choose to be friendly, Tim. That's his problem. I'm glad you chose to be friendly." Mr. Atkins explains carefully about Stop! Think! and Choose! Stop before you act or speak. Think of your options and choose to do what's best for you.

"Well, it's hard to remember to stop when you're mad. My family calls me Temper Tantrum Tim. If I'm mad, I want to hit somebody or throw something. That's my style. What do I do about that?"

"I used to be the same way, Tim. One day I got in big trouble. I hit my big brother. He smashed me back, threw me against the bed and broke my arm. I had a cast on it for weeks—gave me plenty of time to think about losing control."

"How old were you then?"

Mr. Atkins smiles, "I was hoping you wouldn't ask that. I was 17 years old—I should have known better."

In the rest of the one-to-one session they talk about anger and temper tantrums. Mr. Atkins says, "Everyone gets angry once in a while. There are many ways people show anger. No matter how angry a person is, it is not O.K. to hurt someone else. Violent people feel powerful when they hurt others. Their victims feel powerless."

"I really don't want to hit other people, Mr. A., but I'm a moody person and I get mad in a hurry. I don't trust myself not to fly off the handle."

"Let's see if I can help you, Tim." Mr. Atkins writes down a list of suggestions.

- Make sure you have a friend you can talk to when you are upset. Talking can be like blowing off steam. It helps to calm you down.

- Don't blame others when you get mad. Others may do something that causes you to become angry; however, you *choose* whether to become violent. Nobody else makes you act that way.

- Don't hold on to angry feelings because they can build and build. Tell others when you are upset or annoyed and don't keep on adding upsets so that you finally explode in a temper tantrum.

- Sometimes angry people want to be held, talked to, or persuaded to stay in control. Think *"What do I want?"* and tell this to the person with whom you are mad. For example, "I just want you to hold me and not scold me."

- Get in the habit of going to a special *"Time Out"* place where you can calm down. *Choose* to go to that place.

"I'm not sure I can remember those fancy ideas. But I'll try to flash on my *Time Out Chair*. My mom says it's okay to be angry and I know it is."

"Tim, I'll tell you something. When I'm angry—and alone—I *choose* to swear to myself and then I feel better. That helps me. I think of different ways I can get over being mad and swearing works for me."

"Thanks for telling me that. Sometimes I say dirty words under my breath. That's neat that we both do the same thing. Maybe that's because we're getting to be pretty good friends."

"Right on, Tim."

MRS. BRYCE INTRODUCES MARY TO STOP! THINK! AND CHOOSE!

Mary enters Mrs. Bryce's office holding her books against her body—her shoulders are hunched forward and she looks angry. Before the counselor can say anything, Mary says, "This place should be called 'The Prison.' We're not kids. We're prisoners. You can't do anything here. There are so many rules that you can't have any fun at all."

"What's up, Mary?" Mrs. Bryce wants to know.

"I was passing a note to Lisa in Mr. Ryan's room. He saw me—so I tore it up. Then I started to whisper to her and he really got bent out of shape. He told the class, 'This is not the place for gossip. This is the place where I try to teach you some science.' I think it's insulting to a kid to be accused of being a gossip. I was only telling her where to meet me after school. I think Mr. Ryan owes me an apology—don't you?"

As if she didn't hear the question, Mrs. Bryce asks, "Mary—what are you really mad about? What else has happened?" She knows the girl well enough to sense that something more important has occurred.

"Well," Mary begins, "What really made me mad was, after I finished talking to Lisa in the hall—Mr. Ryan came up behind me and said, 'If you'd concentrate as hard on your science as you do on the boys, you'd be a smart person.' I wanted to tell him it was none of his business what I was talking about and thanks for your sarcasm. But I didn't."

"Good for you, Mary. You used good judgment and good control." Mary doesn't hear the compliment.

"I wish I could have told him to shut up.' What's a kid supposed to do when a teacher is insulting—ignore it, smile a phony smile as if you think it is cute? I think those comments should be called 'child abuse.' " She has a faint smile as if her anger has dissipated a bit.

Mrs. Bryce invites her to sit down. "Mary, if you think Mr. Ryan is unreasonable and that you can't talk to him, then don't try. Your next step is to come in here—and I'm glad that you did. What do you think is going on?"

"I think Mr. Ryan is a jerk. I know he's a new teacher and he's got a lot to learn. But he still has no right to make personal remarks to me."

"Maybe he was trying to give you encouragement. 'You'd be a smart person' is a nice remark. You get to *choose* what you hear or how you understand what others say to you."

Mary looks puzzled. "What are you talking about?"

"Most interactions between people come from fear or love. Did you know that?" Mrs. Bryce continues, "You were not paying attention in class. Perhaps Mr. Ryan is afraid he is not a good teacher because he can't keep your attention. So getting 'bent out of shape' is from fear. Maybe he's even afraid he might lose his job."

"Well, why doesn't he say so?"

"Maybe he doesn't even realize it. But let's talk about you. What things do you do that show you are afraid or that you feel loving? Ask yourself some questions: When you are bossy, what do you really feel? When you play around in the halls, what do you really feel? How about when you help your brother with his homework? When you *Stop! Think! and Choose!* to be *mad*—are you *loving* yourself?"

She answers each question thoughtfully. "I guess I'm afraid if I'm not bossy, my friends will go away. They like it. They say, 'Tell us what to do,

Mary. You decide.' I guess I'm afraid I won't get any attention so that's why I play around in the halls. And I help my brother because he needs it. He's not my favorite person, but if I'm going to be a nurse, I might as well learn patience with him."

"I get what you're saying, Mrs. Bryce, but how do you learn to think about fear and love when you're just a kid? If someone trips me in the hall or calls me a name, I don't stop to think those kinds of things."

"When you remember the Stop! Think! and Choose! pattern, add two quick questions. Is this a loving way to treat someone? and What is that person afraid of that makes her talk like that? Is she afraid that I won't notice her or won't be her friend?

"The same questions apply to you. Am I being loving? What am I afraid of that's making me say or do this? There's a book out called *Love Is Letting Go Of Fear** and that's where I learned all this. It works for me, Mary. It's just a way to keep people from getting upset when they don't have to."

"I get it," Mary says. "I'd like to ask you something else. I need braces on my teeth and my mom says we don't have the money. I get mad when I think about my family being poor. What can a kid do? I can Stop! Think! and Choose! all day long and be a good kid, but what about my teeth? If I was rich, I could get them fixed. I guess I'm kinda jealous of rich kids."

"You are asking some heavy-duty questions. Hold on! People like you *for you*, Mary—not because your teeth do or don't need braces. And *you* can like you even if your teeth aren't straight. I had braces when I was 27 years old. I saved the money for a long time. Maybe that's what you'll have to do.

"As for being jealous of rich kids—use your intelligence. Remember, lots of rich kids are unhappy. They may believe money is more important to their parents than they are. One child told me yesterday, 'My dad knows all about the stock market, but he doesn't know my best friend's last name.' Many wish they were as popular and pretty as you are.

"Be happy about who you are, Mary, and concentrate on finding ways to keep from letting anger run your life. We all get angry, but we have to stop and think why we are angry. We can fix some things and some we can't. You can't fix the money situation at your house. Maybe you can help when you're older."

"Okay, Mrs. Bryce. It's time to go. I'll try out this love and fear stuff. Thanks. I'm getting better about asking, 'What else can I say or do?' Maybe I won't let that Mr. Ryan bug me so much anymore."

She mutters, under her breath, "But I deserve some attention from my mom and I don't get it. Maybe she's worried she'll have another heart attack. If she is, why doesn't she talk about it! Maybe I'll ask her."

---

* Gerald Jampolsky, *Love is Letting Go of Fear*, (New York: Bantam Books, 1979).

STEP SIX
POSITIVE MESSAGES ARE IMPORTANT

Background

The give and take of positive messages is an elaboration of Stop! Think! and Choose!

Children Who Hurt have problems with positive messages. Whether deprived as babies or traumatized during early childhood years, they do not believe nice things they are told about themselves. They do not trust affirmations or validation of any kind. As babies, they did not get enough loving positive messages from their parents. This resulted in the fear that no one would take care of them when they needed something. They learned to believe that no one loves them and that they are unlovable. They anticipate that people will be rejecting or hostile towards them. Consequently, they defend themselves by being unfriendly or unloving. They give hostile messages to adults because they mistrust adults. They may also be negative with peers. Among other things, they need to learn how to give and take compliments. (See Appendix, Page 180.)

'Smile and the world smiles with you' is welcome advice for a cheerful person. Children Who Hurt are usually not cheerful and seldom think about how to give a positive message in order to receive a positive message in return.

Because Children Who Hurt habitually and *erroneously* perceive messages from others as unpleasant or hostile, they need help to learn how to stop this bad habit. Help children understand that it is self-defeating and that it does not enhance wellness—rather, it reinforces low self-esteem.

Children need help to understand that one cannot make someone else give positive messages to them. Some parents will rarely, if ever, give their children positive messages. They may be too afraid, depressed, angry or in the habit of being rude. Many people do not know how to say "Thank you" or show love. Explain to children that if they give unfriendly, unloving messages, they are hurting themselves. If the feedback they give is caring, a relationship will get better and better. And then self-acceptance will improve. Also, as they accept positive messages from others, others will want to give them more and more positive messages in return.

If they continue to refuse nice comments or compliments, others will stop saying or doing nice things for them. That may hurt. They may end up lonely.

Use of "I" Messages The *"I" message* is used to state your concerns and feelings in a caring way. When you take responsibility for your own feelings, you model how you want children to take responsibility for theirs. Your positive "I" messages influence children to give positive "I" messages. "Sally, I appreciate your helping Doug with his report. That gave me time to find a film strip to show to the class."

"I" messages are not critical, accusatory, or judgmental. "I can't teach when it is so noisy. I feel frustrated because I have so many interesting things to tell you."

Positive "I" messages promote positive responses. Adult self-disclosure in an office or classroom and in one-to-one sessions should abound in "I" messages. Even if you are angry or disappointed, you can give an "I" message that says that you care. "Mary, when you cry, I would like to comfort you. I would like you to tell me what I can do to help you feel better."

> **Teachers must redefine their role so that facilitation of self-understanding and self-respect becomes a prized function. Self-respect is enhanced when a child learns to give and receive positive feedback.**

For anyone to be positive all the time is unrealistic. Don't expect miracles. However, a person gets to choose. *A person can change.* A person must learn to listen to himself or herself and ask this question, "Would I want someone to talk to me like that?"

For the Child Who Hurts, making an effort to change is a big step. You are urged to reinforce every nice remark that the child makes to you or that you overhear the child saying to others. Each child can learn to *stop* saying negative comments, *think* of positive messages, and *choose* to express them.

Reminders for Adults Reaffirm how valuable you are to the children with whom you are working. You are helping children move toward becoming socially valuable people rather than antisocial. With a renewed sense of self, this transformation can have life-long meaning for many. You can see the eyes of children opening up to the possibility that they are important—that they matter.

Strategies for One-to-One Sessions

Purpose: To understand and stress the importance of positive messages. To clarify how to give and receive positive messages in order to improve communication and relationships. To help a child understand that self-esteem and self-image benefit from positive relationships.

Exercises in Feedback Provide:

- practice in evaluating personal ways of responding to others; a chance to observe one's own good or bad habits.

- lessons on how to verbalize concepts such as "I can *choose* to say or do something pleasant when I give feedback (respond)." "I can't make others respond the way I want, but I can choose what I say and do."

- an awareness of how labels, nicknames, and prejudice affect the feedback you give to others.

- the use of "I" messages.

In one-to-one sessions, Children Who Hurt experience consistent positive messages. The children learn to trust that someone can be consistently accepting.

Directions: Express concepts regarding positive messages. Use your own vocabulary.

Important Statements to Express to a Child Each person gets to choose to be positive or negative.

- "I like what you said or did," is positive.

- "I did not like what you said or did," is negative.

- *Happily, almost everyone can learn to accept and give nice messages.*

- I want to give you consistent acceptance—even if there are times when you are unfriendly or I have been a bit disappointed about something. When you feel accepted consistently, you feel safe. My message to you will always be, "You are special to me. I am here to help you feel better about yourself. If you have a problem, I may assist you as you struggle to straighten things out."

- I will help you understand that you can't make someone else give positive messages to you. Some people may never give positive messages. They may be too afraid, depressed, angry, or in the habit of being rude. Many people do not know how to say "Thank you" or show love.

- If the feedback you give is not friendly or not loving—you hurt yourself by hurting your family or friends. If the feedback you give is caring, a relationship will get better and better.

- If you accept positive messages from others, they will want to give you more and more nice messages. If you do not accept nice messages, including compliments, others will stop saying or doing nice things for you. This may hurt you. You may end up lonely.

You can *choose*. You can change any way you want to change.

Have the child make a copy of the box below and paste it on the outside of a notebook as a ready reminder.

When you give messages, listen to:
- **the words you choose.**
- **what tone of voice you use.**
- **how loudly or softly you speak.**
- **what bodily or facial expressions you show.**

Discuss Negative Messages   Explain that when a person interprets all messages as negative, it is easy for that person to believe:

- I am no good.

- Nobody likes me. I have no friends.

- Nothing will ever get better.

- Nothing good will ever happen to me.

- Nobody understands me.

Negative, Hurtful People   It is hard to remember that it is not your problem if other people do something mean. It shows they feel inferior and are trying to make you feel small.

When others hurt you deliberately, they are trying to control you. They are acting powerful and want you to feel weak. Sometimes this is called victimization.

When another attacks you for something you did not do, the attacker is exhibiting a need to attack.

People who are negative and unfriendly usually do not like themselves.

Tell the child, "You do not have to hurt others. One reason we work together in the one-to-one sessions is to help you like yourself so that *you* will not send negative messages to others."

Remind the child of your promise that you will not pretend you don't know what you know or see what you see. Share negative messages you have observed and recorded on a Struggles Chart. For example, *was nasty to Helen; told Jim to get lost; said "I'm not interested" when Jeff asked him to play.*

Create ways to help the child become aware of habits that need to be changed. Review Activities Pages 5–1 or make up a chart or notebook checklist (using stickers that denote happy, sad, grouchy) on which young children can record how they treat someone else. A child can draw pictures that show unfriendly gestures, him- or herself walking away, pouting, sticking out his or her tongue, and so forth. Older students fill in their Struggles Charts or a journal to collect such information.

Tell the child: "You can learn to change from giving unfriendly messages to giving out friendly messages. You can learn to believe that others want to be friendly."

Continue the practice of expressing a positive greeting at the beginning of each one-to-one session. The greetings become believable as the child learns to trust. By the sixth or seventh session, you may hear a comment that validates your efforts. The child may say, "I like it when you say something nice to me when I come in." Your efforts are beginning to pay off. It is a breakthrough.

Continue the practice of telling stories or incidents in which a child can choose a positive or negative response. Teach positive phrases and actions. Be as specific as you were with Stop! Think! and Choose! Give many examples of nice things to say—friendly greetings, statements which denote empathy, compliments, and so forth.

Ask the child to make a nice remark about anything or anyone that comes to mind. This can be superficial. "I think that boy is wearing a nice sweater." The child may still be reluctant to say anything positive about him- or herself, yet is learning through affirmations.

Teach the child how to defend him- or herself if others are sending negative messages.

Share this list of useful defenses

- Ignore—pretend you don't hear. Become absorbed in a task.

- Walk away.

- Tell the person you don't like what's happening between the two of you: "I'm angry, too," or "I'm hurt by what you say."

For Middle School-age Children

- Tell the person, "Sorry you're angry. I choose not to be the one you throw it at."

- Express anger without hurting someone else. If you have done something wrong, admit it, and try to change what needs to be changed.

- Surprise the person. Tell him or her something you like about him or her.

- Don't pretend not to see what you see or hear what you hear. "I see you looking very mad. Your eyes are squinty. I hear your threats. I am scared. Can we talk?"

Reinforce these statements or defenses with role playing You, the adult, pretend to be angry or hostile. When the child actually acts out these suggested defenses—even in play—the words and phrases begin to feel familiar.

The child may scoff and say, "That sounds stupid," or, "I don't talk like that," or "Why should I learn to say nice things if the other kids don't say nice things to me?" Encourage the child to try out these defenses with classmates or members of the family. Have him or her tell you about the experiences.

Teach how to give "I" messages Explain about "owning" feelings and guarding against angry, critical or accusatory remarks.

Discuss items from Activity 6–1

End of the Session

Set the time for the next one-to-one session.

End with an optimistic personal statement such as, "I'm looking forward to seeing you again. I'm sure we can. . . ."

Use affirmations. Repeat instructions as often as necessary.

SHELLY AND MISS TIPTON DISCUSS POSITIVE MESSAGES

When Shelly comes in to talk, she starts by saying, "I've got something to tell you. When I woke up this morning, I decided to be nice to everybody

(Continued on page 101)

POSITIVE MESSAGES ARE IMPORTANT

Directions: Read the statements below. Fill in the blanks.

Reminders:
There are no right or wrong answers.
Handwriting and spelling don't count.
All answers are confidential.

It is nice when you can depend on a friend to be friendly, even if you are in a bad mood. It makes people feel sad or worried or mad if they act friendly to someone and the person does not respond in a friendly way. Positive messages are very important, but no one can be positive all the time.

Feedback is what other people say or do in response to what you have said or done. You can't make a person respond to you in any special way; for example, you can try to make somebody laugh but it may not happen. You *can* try to predict how another will respond to the messages you send, especially if you have a close relationship with the other person.

If you do something friendly and others act friendly back, that's the kind of feedback that you will like. Some friendly things that you can do are _____

_____

_____

_____

Some positive messages may be
___ smiles   ___ touches   ___ explanations
___ laughs   ___ questions or comments about
___ caring "I" messages   what you are sharing.

People like others to notice them and answer when they talk to them. When they are ignored or nobody pays attention to them, it can hurt their feelings. If you are in this situation, what can you do? How would you feel?

_____

_____

Here are some answers to this question that other students have made up. What do you think of these answers? I would:

ask for what I want.

act as if it doesn't matter. Ignore it.

figure out that what I have to
  say is not important or interesting.

do something silly to get
  attention.

get mad and show that I am mad.

choose to believe that people don't like
  me.

Activity 6–1, continued

Some people feel that others react to them or give them negative or positive messages because of their size, color, talents, or nicknames. For example, you think one of your classmates is "dumb" yet he/she asks you a reasonable question. "Do you think it will rain this afternoon?" Your answer: "How do I know, Dummy?" If someone else asked the same question, you might answer, "Look at those clouds. They call those rain clouds."

What is your reaction to these names or labels?

Brainy	Shorty	Uptown Kid
Dummy, Stupid	Slow Poke	Jock
Giant	Perfectionist	Cowboy
Know-it-all	Class Clown	Teacher's Pet

_____

_____

For each person, certain feedback or responses are easy to give and some are not. Some make us feel good, others bad. Complete the following sentences. These are positive situations.

When I tell Harry a good story, I like it when he says _____

_____

_____

I lend Jenny my bike. When she brings it back, I'd like her to say _____

_____

_____

I broke my mom's dish by mistake. I said I'm sorry. I'd like to hear her say

_____

_____

Positive things that are easy for me to say are

_____

_____

Positive things that are hard for me to say are

_____

_____

> **Speak kind words and you will hear kind echoes**
> **(Unknown)**

today. When I got to school and said, 'Hi, Megan,' she didn't answer me. She wasn't nice at all."

"That was a good start, Shelly. I guess Megan needs more than one friendly greeting in order to be sure that you want to be her friend."

"Maybe she'll never be friendly," Shelly says as she picks up some clay.

"There are many ways to show someone that you like them. Each is a *positive message*. Let's pretend that you and I are acting on a stage. You be friendly to me and let's see what happens."

Shelly says, "That might be fun, but it's just a game, and in real life you are already nice to me." She makes a lollipop out of clay and hands it to Miss Tipton who is pretending to be a little girl.

"Thanks. I like lollipops, but I don't have time to play with you now."

Shelly tries again. She makes a ball out of clay and throws it at the teacher. The "pretend" little girl catches the ball. "Good throw, Shelly, but I'm too tired to play ball."

Shelly asks, "Why isn't that girl more friendly yet?"

Miss Tipton explains, "She's not sure you want to be friendly—maybe you just want attention. I like what you're doing in this make-believe theater. Keep it up. Pretty soon that other girl will believe your messages and be nicer."

Shelly makes a clay pencil. The "other girl" says thanks, but she doesn't need one. Shelly makes a clay orange. The "other girl" isn't hungry. Shelly makes a clay doll. Miss Tipton, as the other girl, is happy. "I like dolls. Thanks. Can we play dolls together?" The "other girl" grins. Then she adds, "I guess you really want to be friends, Shelly. I'm glad."

Miss Tipton explains again about positive messages. She reads the five messages listed below and asks Shelly to select the positive ones.

When a person smiles at you, you may:

give eye-to-eye contact

run away

pretend you don't care

smile

frown

Shelly's choices are right. "I get it!," she says.

Miss Tipton explains patiently that some people get in the habit of saying or doing unfriendly things. They may also mistakenly think that others are being unfriendly when that is not so. She asks, "Has this ever happened to you?"

Shelly doesn't answer the question but slips in a remark. "Maybe sometimes I act mad when I'm not. When I think people are unfriendly, I get mad. Now I understand that I sometimes have to do *a lot* of things before someone believes that I want to be their friend."

Miss Tipton decides to go one step further with the discussion. "Shelly, give yourself an important affirmation and say 'I'm a nice person. I deserve friends.' "

Shelly ignores the suggestion. "I wish Megan would come to my house to see my Barbie. I get lonely. I never told that to anyone before."

Miss Tipton smooths Shelly's hair and presses her fingers gently on the back of Shelly's neck. "I like you, Shelly." To herself, she muses, "I believe she is learning to trust."

As Shelly gets up to leave, she asks if she could keep a tiny bit of clay in her pocket. She says, "It will remind me to give out positive messages."

"Of course, honey," Miss Tipton says, "and don't forget your affirmations."

ROGER AND MRS. SNYDER DISCUSS POSITIVE MESSAGES

Mrs. Snyder sits at her desk, and Roger stands next to her staring at the blackboard.

"I'm not in the mood to talk to you today," he says. "I wish I could go home and watch TV. Then I don't have to be bothered by anybody—even you."

"What's happened, Roger? You've never talked to me like that before."

"I'm sick of being a *nobody*. At home I can tell my dad something and he says, 'Yeah. So what?' I tell my mom something and she says, 'I'm too busy to hear about your problem. You're going to be ten years old. You're old enough to figure things out.' I was only telling them about Jason and Mike and how they tease me. Yesterday those boys hid my lunch. Today they took my mittens."

"Why are they teasing you, Roger?"

"I dunno. Maybe they just want to see me get mad."

"What did you do when they took your things?"

"I called them dumb and grabbed my stuff. When I did, Jason said, 'I think your face would break if you ever smiled—and you don't even get really mad. What's the matter with you? Are you for real?' and then he walked off."

"Roger, there are times when you seem to be in a world of your own. You don't laugh or get mad. You don't seem sad either. You're just there—watching the others. Maybe the boys want you to *respond* to them. They want you to show your feelings."

"Well, at my house *no one* shows any feelings to me. You're the only one who smiles at me, but you smile at the other kids, too."

Mrs. Snyder said, "We need to talk more about positive and negative feedback, Roger." She presents him with the Activities Pages. She reads, *People like others to notice them and answer them when they talk. When they are ignored or nobody pays attention to them, it can hurt their feelings. If you were in that situation, what would you do? How would you feel?* Roger and Mrs. Snyder read over the list of possible answers.

- ask for what I want

- do something silly to get attention

- act as if it doesn't matter. Ignore it.

- get mad and show that I am mad

- figure out that what I have to say is not important or interesting

- choose to believe that people don't like me

Roger says, "I just act as if it doesn't matter—that's what I always do."

Mrs. Snyder picks up on his comment. "Roger, when these boys tease you, they want you to respond to them. I think they really want to know you better. Maybe they tease you to get you to change and be more friendly. Kids do that sometimes."

"Why would they want me to be more friendly?"

"Because you're a nice guy, and you were funny in the play yesterday. Maybe they'd like to see you act funny again."

Mrs. Snyder suggests that they look over the list of possible answers again and write them in two columns.

Positive	*Negative*
Ask for what I want	Do something silly to get attention
	Act as if it doesn't matter
	Get mad and show that I am mad
	Figure out that what I have to say is not important or interesting
	Choose to believe that people don't like me

Mrs. Snyder says, "Only one positive answer, Roger? Let's make up some more positive things one could say in that situation."

- "Ask others to listen while you repeat what you said, 'Perhaps you didn't hear me. I'll tell you again.' "

- "If what I said was boring, please tell me. I'll try to be more interesting or talk about different things."

- "Give an 'I' message. 'I'm sorry that you didn't say anything when told you about the dream I had last night. It was scary. I needed to tell someone.' "

- " 'If I have repeated myself, please tell me. I'll try to remember what I've already told you.' Make positive statements, Roger, whenever you can. You can't make others answer or make sure that they will be positive. You can only be in charge of you."

When you are positive, you usually get positive feedback.

"It takes time to learn that you are okay—even if you don't get positive responses from others when you want them. But, Roger, your first job is to make sure that *you* give positive messages. You tend to express negative thoughts or criticisms about yourself and other people, too."

Roger changes the subject. "Why are you nice to everybody? Why can't you be especially nice to me?"

"What would you like me to do? How can I show you that you are special to me?"

"Nobody has ever called me 'Bud.' I like that name. I hate the name Roger. Will you call me 'Bud' when we talk?"

"Good plan, Bud. Thanks for asking for what you'd like."

"I want to talk about my parents. They aren't positive with me."

"That's not your fault, Roger. You tell me that they don't give you the hugs you want. You have to choose. Accept them the way they are—as nonhuggers—or ask for what you want with words."

"They won't change, Mrs. Snyder. They'll always be like statues with me. The only time my dad acts excited is when he's drunk. Even then, Mom walks around as if she is just watching him. We are all *watchers*. I guess that's what people do when they live with someone who drinks too much."

"Bud, at school watchers can be lonely. Let's go back to the Activities Pages and look at this. *If you do something friendly and others act friendly back, that's the kind of feedback that you will like. Some friendly things that you can do are. . . .*

"Write down some answers and we'll talk about positive feedback again. Okay, Bud?" she says as she hugs him and helps him put on his jacket.

He says quietly, "I deserve friends because I don't fight, and I know three jokes that are pretty funny. The other kids might like to hear them," he mentions as he leaves.

TIM AND MR. ATKINS DISCUSS POSITIVE MESSAGES

"I'm the tallest kid in this class and I hate it. The kids call me 'Bean Pole.' It makes me mad that I'm tall and still can't play decent basketball. And this scar on my face—once in a while people bug me about it. They ask, 'What did you do, Tim, walk into a door?' "

Tim continues talking about himself. Mr. Atkins perceives that—he really seems to be learning to trust.

Tim continues, "I never know what to say when kids tease me. My height is my big problem. It's like they expect me to be a great athlete and the girls say dumb things like, 'He's gonna be a hunk.' That's really stupid because they can see that I'm skinny and these new glasses aren't cool."

Mr. Atkins reassures the boy, "I was the tallest kid in my class, too, Tim, and I liked it. I got to stand in the back in the class picture and I could grab the hats off the heads of the short guys and toss them away. They'd get so mad. In high school tall *was* great with the girls. Hang in there, Tim. You'll find out."

"I think kids just see me as someone tall. They don't even know me. I hate it," Tim says.

Mr. Atkins says, "How would you like people to treat you? Lots of times people react to us because of what we look like or something like that instead of who we are as a person. It's called prejudice—responding to body size, color, or sex, and not the person. That's what the girls complain about when they say, 'Oh, that's a male chauvinist remark' or 'He's being a macho man.' "

"It's important for kids to be able to talk about themselves, to describe themselves to other people so that they don't hide behind nicknames or labels that hurt. 'Shorty,' 'Bean Pole,' 'Scarface,' 'Dimples,' 'Big Mouth,' 'Fatso' and 'Brainy' are examples of this."

Mr. Atkins continues. "Even if people call you a name like 'Bean Pole,' you get to *choose* how you respond—what kind of feedback to give." He explains that feedback is made up of two parts: messages you give others and the messages others give you. "I'd like to help you see if you give negative or positive messages. Sometimes we give unfriendly messages without realizing it."

The phone rings and Mr. Atkins makes an appointment to see a parent at five o'clock. "That mother was sweet. She wants to help her son, but the son won't even speak to her. Now she's coming to school after work just to get some ideas on what to do that might make him act nicer to her."

Tim suggests, "Help her figure out if she is always on the kid's back. She may be sweet to you, Mr. Atkins, but maybe she's not sweet at home. People can sure change fast or be phony.

"Talking about that mom and her kid made me think of something.

Whenever my mom says anything nice to me, I tell her to 'cool it' or I ask her 'What do you want?' How come when you say something nice to me, I don't tell you to cool it?"

Mr. Atkins answers, "You get to *choose how you hear things*, Tim."

They talk about the give and take of positive messages. Mr. Atkins is consistently positive while Tim's mother mixes nice statements with so many put-downs that Tim doesn't even listen to her.

Tim and the teacher make up positive endings for the positive situations on the Activities Pages. Tim has a wry expression on his face as he admits, "I guess I'm not much for this positive stuff." Before he leaves, Tim comments, "I may be a 'Bean Pole' at school and sort of a Mr. Nobody at home, but I'm beginning to believe you really like me. It's about time, isn't it?"

"It takes time, Tim." The two exchange smiles as the boy leaves.

MARY AND MRS. BRYCE DISCUSS POSITIVE MESSAGES

Mary is late for her appointment with Mrs. Bryce. She looks tired. She slumps into a chair and asks, "Well, what do we have to talk about today?"

"I guess I don't hear much love in that question, Mary. What's happening with you?"

Mary begins talking about three things that make her mad: the put-downs from Mr. Ryan, the two girls who told her off, and her mom who made her clean her room Saturday afternoon. She didn't get to meet her friends at the mall.

"Sounds to me as if you went from one situation to another and ended up feeling as if you didn't have much power. Do you have any idea why all of this is happening at one time?"

"I can't think of a decent thing that's happened to me in a long time. I'm in a bad mood. I don't care if Mr. Ryan likes me or not. It's no big deal. If the girls don't want to do what I want to do, they can get lost. And as for my mom, she thinks she's a big shot because she can boss me around."

Mrs. Bryce picks up on the "bad mood" comment and talks about the tendency for teenagers to be moody. "Everybody gets that way. It's when you want the world to leave you alone. You get the feeling that everyone is your enemy. You give out the message, 'Stay out of my way.' "

Mary says, "I wanted to try some pot to see if maybe I'd feel better, but I didn't. My cousin likes pot. He gets it from a friend. It doesn't cost very much. I'd never tell anyone but you that that's what I was thinking about."

Mrs. Bryce is glad to hear this statement: it indicates that Mary is trusting her a bit.

"Mary, you're too nice a person to get involved with pot. It is *not* an okay thing to do to help you get out of a bad mood."

Mrs. Bryce points to a poster she has on the wall, *Good Things To Say To Yourself.*

"Why do I have that there? What does it mean to you?"

Mary is not very polite. "It's just a sign to make kids think about thinking in a positive way. It's not my style."

"Let's try something else, Mary. I'll pretend to put you down. I want you to come back at me."

Mrs. Bryce: "That sweater's too big for you. It looks weird."

Mary: "Big deal. Who cares? What's it to you?"

Mrs. Bryce: "You play volleyball like a nearsighted goose."

Mary: "Thanks for the compliment. I figured that out for myself. Besides, I hate gym."

Mrs. Bryce: "If you ever said anything nice about anybody, I'd faint. I think you broke your 'smiler' a year ago."

Mary: "I thought you'd never notice."

Mrs. Bryce stops the game. "You are a master at sarcasm, Mary. Let's go with 'up' statements instead."

"That sounds boring. I can think of nice things if I want to. There's nothing nice going on in my life right now."

Mrs. Bryce hands Mary a paper entitled *Positive Self-Talk.* The instructions were to write down nice comments about oneself. With much coaxing from her counselor, Mary writes:

I look okay.	I am honest.
I have friends.	I like my hair.
I make some good decisions.	I am an okay cook.
I can get good grades if I try.	

"That's an okay list, but it's not so easy to think upbeat thoughts when you're mad," Mary says.

"I agree, Mary, but you're the one who can choose the negative or the positive. Remember, if someone tries to put you down, it's that person's problem."

"Well, it doesn't *feel* that way," Mary protests. "But I'll think about it."

"Mary, when you feel rotten, *give yourself positive feedback.* Say to yourself, 'Things are in a mess. I'm mad *but I am okay*' or 'My mom ticks me off—*but I am okay.*' 'I goofed when I didn't get my room cleaned earlier, but *everybody goofs now and then*'. Giving yourself positive feedback is a great habit to get into. It beats putting yourself down, smoking pot, drinking, or any other fixer-upper."

They look over the items on the Activities Pages. Mary lightens up a bit and makes several funny remarks. They both smile as they schedule their next appointment and state affirmations.

Mrs. Bryce runs her fingers through her hair as she tells Mary, "I enjoy our visits. Mary, maybe you have forgotten that you are special to me." The girl looks up and says, "Then I guess I must be okay."

With a twinkle in her eye, Mary says, "You must have taken your Happy Pills today, Mrs. Bryce. Guess I'll try some tomorrow. I deserve some. See you later. Thanks," and she leaves for class.

STEP SEVEN
HELP BOTH THE CHILD AND YOURSELF END ONE-TO-ONE SESSIONS

Background and Strategies

The end of a Trust Building Program may be painful for you and the child. It may also be a celebration. The bond between you is mutually rewarding. The child has indeed become special to you.

When Is It Time to End the Program?   This is perhaps the most difficult of all questions to answer. The Child Who Hurts has a myriad of needs. There is always much more you could do to help. However, in the course of the fourteen to twenty one-to-one sessions, you have touched on a number of important points. You have focused on the core problem—the child's learning to trust *you*—plus numerous ways to enhance self-esteem. You have observed improvements. You have noted that some symptoms of hurt have diminished or disappeared. You may want to use three documents to support your decision to end the one-to-one sessions. These three documents are: the *Struggles Charts*, the *Indicators of Healthy Self-Esteem*, and *Statements That Denote a Child Has Learned to Trust*. You have your Struggles Charts already. The other two documents follow.

Indicators of Healthy Self-Esteem

Is self-accepting	Takes time to be creative
Sets goals	Can trust others
Accepts talents and skills	Is free from a victim role
Chooses solitude on occasion	Recognizes defeatist or nonproductive attitudes and
Maintains a positive body image	wants to let let them go
Is reflective at times	Enjoys life

Statements That Denote a Child Has Learned to Trust

Now I can believe that a grownup will be my friend—even if I have a bad day.

I really get mixed up. My mom calls me stupid, but you never do. I'm beginning to see that *I can* learn and do better in school.

Now I can believe it when you tell me that something is *not* my fault.

I must be a little "okay" because you meet with me alone—because you *want* to. I used to see teachers alone because I did something wrong.

When you tell me about you—that makes me feel special. I hear you talk about yourself in class, but you tell me different things and I like that.

Something neat happened to me yesterday. I got invited to a birthday party. I thought about you right away. I think you have helped me to be nicer to the other kids. You must really like me—to explain so many times about being friendly.

Weigh your assessment against two other considerations—the amount of time you have devoted to this child and the neediness of other children who might benefit from your help. If you are reasonably satisfied with the progress that has been made, it is time to terminate. Your judgment, plus your observations, are what count. *Remember, a Trust Building Program is an important beginning and the child will recall and use what you have discussed.* Together you will discuss plans for possible future meetings and greetings.

A Plan to End the Program   Discontinuing one-to-one meetings may be difficult. When you tell the child, "We will meet only 2 or 3 more times," it may result in a marked increase in the child's anxiety. This anxiety may be displayed as anger. The child may clam up, be openly hostile, refuse to come to any sessions or act-out in class. Two questions emerge in the child's mind: "Can I make it without you?" and "Will you still care for me even if we don't get to talk?"

During these final sessions, take every precaution to prevent feelings of rejection or abandonment. Be positive.

"I know you can keep up the good work. You know it, too."

"I may not see you in one-to-one sessions, but you are still special to me."

"I've noticed you have new friends. I'm proud of you."

Ending The Program Is a Vote of Confidence   In the final one-to-one sessions, *review improvements.* Do Activity 7–1. Read over the collection of Struggles Charts that now abound in positive observations. Both of you may have written, "Greeted others as got off the bus," "Volunteered for committee work," "More relaxed today," "Laughed a lot at lunch." (If you haven't collected

Struggles Charts or kept other notes, you can brainstorm improvements together readily.)

Select some items from Indicators of Healthy Self-Esteem and the Trust Statements to talk about. These may sound like compliments, and the child may still discount what you say. Be prepared for statements such as, "Well, that's not much," or, "It probably won't last," or, "I can only do it if you help me." Don't dwell on these negative remarks. Each may be a plea for the continuation of the one-to-one work, and it is time for the child to branch out on his or her own.

If you are in a school setting, reassure the child that you will see each other—perhaps in class. "You know that I discuss, in my groups or class, many of the same ideas that we have talked about in private. These discussions will help you. For example, everyone will hear *Stop! Think! and Choose!* or be told how to ask for *Facts.* Similar comments would be appropriate in anticipation of meetings in a 4-H or Church group.

Set a Cut-off Date   When the child accepts that the sessions will end, that you will only have one or two more sessions, he or she may be motivated to do very well, or do something special to please you. This contrasts with the initial negative behaviors that have followed your announcement that the program would end soon.

A cut-off date is evidence of the confidence you have in the child. It validates your observations. It is a *limit.*

Design a Follow-up Plan

Designate what future follow-up you would welcome   There must be future contacts and conversations; not one-to-one sessions as such. The Child Who Hurts needs these contacts to look forward to. If you are a mentor, 4-H leader, or the like, you will probably be seeing each other on a regular basis. Counselors, teachers, social workers, or psychologists may have to schedule contacts.

Some ideas that you might consider:

Schedule a phone call once a week (set a time and day).

Have the child stop in before school every other Friday (or alternate day).

Have the child hand in ongoing completed Struggles Charts for you to read.

Offer to exchange encouraging notes—reminders of sayings, slogans, phrases, and so forth.

> The child needs periodic checkups. These can be most reward-ing to you, too.

Be certain that you do not suggest a plan that you may not be able to keep.
At the end of the school year, it is a temptation to suggest regular reunions such as, "Let's meet at the town pool on Thursday afternoons." It's best not to do this because there are many Thursdays and impromptu conflicting plans may make the reunions impossible.
A disappointment after a time lapse may rekindle doubts and self-depreciation. It may reawaken thoughts that grownups are not to be trusted.

Disclosures to New Teachers   If the Program is terminated at the end of the semester or school year, decide together what facts the child wants you to share with new teachers, counselors, aides, coaches, or whomever. The information to the child's new teachers about talents, problems, interests *and improvements* can be very useful. Children with problems may be reluctant to talk about difficulties, yet want their new teachers to be informed. They do not want to repeat material they have already mastered.
The student may want *you* to convey the information. No problem!
Notes in the child's school record may be ignored or there may be no place to report progress in the social or emotional areas. Some districts do not want such notations; however, a "receiving teacher" may be grateful for the information.

Express Feelings   In your final meeting, allow a lot of time for students to express their feelings. You know the children well. You know how they express feelings. Some may express appreciation and devotion, dependency and love. Others may be reticent—even silent or angry. A few may cry.
Be very open with your feelings. Give "I" messages. "I will miss our visits together," "I want to know how you are getting along. I'll be disappointed if you don't keep in touch," "I'm very proud of you."

> You cannot fix parent-child relationships. It's not your job.

After The Program   *Keep your expectations realistic.* These children have had their problems for years before you began working with them. They will still have to confront painful situations and difficult relationships. Even with improved or new social skills and a stronger self-image, crises will invariably arise.

If a crisis occurs at home. You may be the only person a child trusts enough to turn to for help. He or she may need your objective comments, advice, and support. Reassure the child that he or she is not to blame.

Remind the child to Stop! Think! and Choose! and that he or she can make good decisions. One decision may be to control what he or she says and does.

If a crisis occurs at school. The child may fall apart or get caught in a very upsetting situation at a time when you are out of the building or unavailable for other reasons. You are not there to support and protect the child, and consequently the child may feel betrayed. When you have an opportunity, explain why you were not available at the time. The child may ask, "How come I used to be important to you and I'm not any more?" Don't be defensive. Tell the truth. "You are important and I'm sorry I could not come when you needed me."

If you are available, see the child in person and be as supportive as possible. Listen and empathize. Help the child recognize appropriate behaviors and evidences of wellness. Discuss weaknesses which may have contributed to the crisis. *Under certain circumstances, it may be advisable to start one-to-one sessions again.* If you do, structure with set limits. "I will see you three times." Mention the possibility of referring to others for help, if necessary, such as protective services or a medical professional.

You have discontinued a program; you have not disconnected from this person. You have formed a strong, valuable bond that may be essential to the child's continuing development.

Reflections . . . As you reflect on your work with Children Who Hurt, acknowledge that you could not solve many of the problems that the children must still face. You instead introduced *trust.* You helped them learn to manage their behavior. You helped repair damaged self-esteem.

- Don't sell yourself short.

- Don't underestimate the power of your care. Be proud of what you have done for Children Who Hurt.

- Reaffirm your effectiveness. See how many goals of the Trust Building Program you were able to achieve.

Be pleased that you helped each child understand that he or she is lovable.

**You have enriched your life as a person.
The child will never forget you.**

ENDING ONE-TO-ONE SESSIONS

Directions: Read the statements. Fill in the blanks.

Reminders:
There are no right or wrong answers.
Handwriting and spelling don't count.
All answers are confidential.

These activities pages are important. Please write down your thoughts about o
program and what it has meant to you. Your answers will help you appreciate ho
much you have learned and the variety of things that we have talked about. This w
be positive feedback from *you to you.*

Most kids have mixed emotions when they start one-to-one sessions. My feeling
were

_____

_____

_____

Now I feel _____

_____

_____

I have heard the word *trust* repeatedly. Now trust, to me, means

_____

_____

_____

In the sessions, you have spent time with a grownup who likes you a lot. This pers
has shared a lot with you. Perhaps you consider this grownup a friend. Describe ho
this feels.

_____

_____

_____

As a result of your one-to-one sessions, in what ways have you changed with yo
friends? Have you made new friends?

_____

_____

You have learned about affirmations; their importance, and how to give them to yourself. What are your favorite affirmations today?

Now and then everyone has to deal with disappointments and upsetting situations. What have you learned about managing yourself when something upsetting happens in your life? Have you learned to think about *Stop! Think! and Choose?* Has it become a habit? It can, you know—with a lot of practice.

In one-to-one sessions we have talked a lot about relationships—getting along with other people. Can you think of any special suggestions that you liked the best or were easiest to try? Which have been the hardest or not yet possible?

We have discussed a lot of facts about you (learning problems, low self-esteem, being gifted and talented, etc.) Is there anyone you would like me to share this information with?

You knew from the beginning that the Trust Building Program would only be for a few weeks. In what ways would you like to keep in touch? What special words of encouragement would you like to hear?

If a crisis should come up, please don't hesitate to ask for help.

SHELLY AND MISS TIPTON MEET FOR THE LAST TIME

Shelly is wearing a flowered blouse and new pink cordoroy pants. She looks cheerful. She smiles a soft smile as she approaches Miss Tipton.

"I've got something nice to tell you. Last night my cousin came over and I told her about you. She asked me if she could meet you and I said, 'No, I'm sorry—she's *my* teacher—and she's my friend, too.' I thought maybe you'd like to know that I said that."

"That makes me happy, Shelly. I'm glad you feel that way. You certainly have changed. I'm proud of you. When we first met, you were afraid of me—and now you're not afraid anymore. The last time we met, I told you that we weren't going to have our special meetings anymore, but we would visit occasionally *and* still be together every day in class. Don't be afraid, Shelly, that I won't be your friend anymore. You will always be special to me."

"Tell me again why we aren't going to meet."

"You are a happier person now. You have learned to share with me and you have friends. You are doing well with your work. I know that I haven't been able to answer all your questions—especially about your mother, but perhaps you understand about asking for the facts you want.

"We aren't going to meet because I must spend the time with others who need me. Don't worry. I won't talk about you, and what you have shared with me is as safe as ever."

Shelly reaches out and gently touches Miss Tipton on the arm. "You're a nice lady," she says, "and I'm going to write you a letter on my new stationery that my grandmother bought me. It's got flowers on it—like my blouse. What are your favorite flowers?"

"I like roses and forget-me-nots."

"I do, *too*," the little girl says. With a serious expression on her face, she says, "I'd like it if you were friends with my daddy. Then maybe you could be my new mommie."

"Thanks, Shelly, but we are friends only at school. But if your daddy should get married again, I know you will learn to be friends with your stepmother. In the meantime, enjoy living with your Grammie. She loves you a lot."

"I know it," Shelly says, "But I'll miss our talks."

"I will, too," her teacher says as they walk hand in hand toward the door.

ROGER AND MRS. SNYDER MEET FOR THE LAST TIME

Roger enters the room looking dejected. "Last time we met, you said this would be our last session. Did you really mean that?" Timidly, Roger raises his eyes.

"Yes, Bud, but you will always be special to me, and I have enjoyed every talk we have had. I'm proud of every improvement you've made, and I am happy that you shared with me. You are stronger now. Your attitude has changed a lot. You seem more cheerful, and I've noticed you and Fred have become good friends. There are other students who need time alone with me— and that's one reason why I'm discontinuing our meetings. I will still see you every day in class, and we can occasionally find time to talk for a short while. You've finished the Activities Pages and have done a good job, I might add."

Roger acts as if he isn't a bit impressed with what Mrs. Snyder has to say. He changes the subject. "Well, I still make a lot of mistakes, and I still need you to help me. I missed five spelling words today, and I studied them last night. I asked my dad to help me, but he was watching TV. He said, 'After the game is over, kid,' but by that time I was asleep."

"Bud, stop it. Stop criticizing yourself, and stop blaming other people. It is okay to make mistakes. I've told you that before. *It is not okay for you to be so critical of yourself.* When you make a mistake, you may feel upset or embarrassed or discouraged. But you can get over it. You have to learn to say to yourself: 'Bud, it is not awful to make a mistake,' or 'Bud, stop telling yourself that you are not okay because you make mistakes.' Stop telling yourself 'I'll never get this right,' or 'I can never win.'"

She opens her desk and hands Roger a paper. "I just happen to have this handy, Bud. Let's make some cards for you to put in your notebook. You choose the sentences from this page that you like best." She gives him cards and a black magic marker to use.

Roger chooses three statements from a page entitled, *It's Okay To Make a Mistake.*

Everybody makes mistakes. I'll just try again.

I'll see if I can do better next time.

I feel bad, but it's not the end of the world.

He puts the cards in his pocket. "I like you a lot, Mrs. Snyder. You make me feel important. I've never said anything like that to anyone in my whole life." He smiles a faint smile, looks down at the floor, and then says just above a whisper, "I guess I deserve to have my teacher like me cause I'm an okay kid," and he leaves.

TIM AND MR. ATKINS MEET FOR THE LAST TIME

Mr. Atkins looks across his desk at Tim who is unusually calm. The teacher waits for the boy to start their conversation.

"You told me about put-downs and how you protect yourself so they don't hurt so much. I'm no good at that. I still get mad and want to do the person one better. Will I ever be able to stop that? And how am I gonna do it now that you're not going to see me anymore?" He sounds as if he were pleading with Mr. Atkins to continue the one-to-one talks. Mr. Atkins answers, "Tim, you can be in charge of you—how you act *and* what you think. You can turn on a pretend tape recorder in your head that repeats one question: Tim, are you taking care of you? and answer that in an upbeat way. You know what I mean, don't you?"

"No, I don't. That sounds like nothing to me."

"Okay, let's start again. You have kept a Struggles Chart for weeks. Both of us have noticed a lot of nice things you have done, and many times you've been well-controlled—not a single temper tantrum in school. So now you're upset about what others say, Tim. Don't believe everything you hear about yourself. You can compare yourself to others and see your own strong and weak points. You can decide that you can work on your weak points if you want to.

"Tim, why not start to do more things with other kids? You call yourself a loner; maybe it's time to join a group—even try out for a team. It helps to be part of a group. When you spend too much time alone, you tend to get sensitive and to imagine that other people are saying or thinking unkind things about you—and that's not true."

Tim picked up a basketball from the corner of the room. He threw it in the wastebasket. "I'd never make a team, Mr. A, you know that. But I would like to do a project with some other guys. I can draw pretty well. I could paint some banners for the gym for the game next Saturday and a bunch of us could hang them up."

"That's a good place to start."

Tim pitches the ball into the basket again. "But what about not talking to you?"

"I see you as a more confident boy than you used to be. How about continuing to keep your Struggles Chart? Put it on my desk once a week, and I'll find time to talk to you about it. It just won't be fifteen or twenty minutes like we've been having."

"That sounds pretty good," the boy admits. "And, one more thing, my mom says she wants me to have a *big brother*—some man who would take me to the zoo or some dumb thing like that. Doesn't that sound dumb to you? I like helping that girl with her math, and you've kinda been like a big brother, but I think this new thing is stupid." He scrunches a piece of paper into a ball and throws it in the basket. He runs his fingers through his hair. He is glum. Tim mutters, "Don't answer that. I know I'm just off the wall because I won't be seeing you a lot any more."

Mr. Atkins walks over to Tim. "I'd like to give you a hug, Tim. I want to tell you, you are a good kid."

Tears well up in Tim's eyes. "I've never had a man give me a hug. I watch other kids when their dads hug them, and they say, 'Hey, quit it,' but that's something I've never had." He approaches his teacher—stands close to him and says, "You really do make me feel special. Thanks, Mr. A." The teacher presses his fingers into Tim's shoulders, and the boy smiles as he picks up his books to leave.

MARY AND MRS. BRYCE MEET FOR THE LAST TIME

Mary saunters into the office carrying a flower in her hand. She hands it to Mrs. Bryce. "I found this in the street on the way to school, and I thought you might like to have it."

"Thank you, Mary." The counselor can tell that Mary is reaching out and holding back at the same time. "I'm delighted with my chrysanthemum."

"Well, I decided that you've helped me understand a bunch of things, and that was nice of you. Is this really the last time I'll come in your office for these one-to-one talks? I used to hate coming here, but now I kinda like it."

Mrs. Bryce reassures her, "You are always welcome to come here on an appointment basis, Mary, but these special sessions end today. You seem happier and less angry. That's what it was all about. I'll give you your Activities Pages so you can look them over whenever you want. They are good reminders of what we have talked about. By the way, I have a new paper that I thought might be of interest to you." She takes out a *Things About Me That Need Work* checklist and explains that it is an assortment of statements to help people feel good about themselves. "Let's look this over together. I want you to feel empowered to use your personality and talents to make sure that you have happy relationships and happy times."

"This sounds like a lot," Mary says as they start to read the items.

Things About Me That Need Work

	YES With Whom	NEEDS WORK With Whom
I communicate well with other people.	_____	_____
I am satisfied with how I take responsibilities at home.	_____	_____
I am satisfied with how I take responsibility for my school work.	_____	_____
I am pleased with my relationships with my friends.	_____	_____

I am pleased with my relationships with my father/mother/sister/brother.	_____	_____
I am a good listener.	_____	_____
I find it easy to express my true feelings.	_____	_____
I am pleased at how I spend my time.	_____	_____
I can talk to my friends about anything.	_____	_____
I am reliable about keeping secrets, being on time, and showing loyalty.	_____	_____
I am a good money manager.	_____	_____
I have ideas or plans about my future.	_____	_____

After they read over the items, Mrs. Bryce says, "I want to encourage you to keep your goal of becoming a pediatric nurse. It will take lots of patience and understanding, but Mary, you know that understanding begins with *knowing who you are,* and you're learning a lot about you. I'm proud of you."

Mary is pensive. She looks out the window as she says, "But I still like to have the others let me be the boss. I still like to be different than most of the girls. I think they are cutesy, and I'm not impressed. But I am glad you've helped me think about telling the truth and being more careful about what I say and do. I can't talk to my mom; you know that. But I will come by and talk to you."

"Oh," she says as she turns around, "My report card came yesterday and I got the best grades I've ever had. Mom didn't say anything, but my brother asked, 'Hey, what happened? Did you cheat?' Just like him." She is not upset. She seems self-assured, and in her perky, pretty manner, she waves goodbye.

4 HOW TO USE THE CONCEPTS OF A TRUST BUILDING PROGRAM WITH A GROUP

Teachers have their students. Counselors conduct groups and sometimes work with classes. Youth leaders meet with various-sized groups in assorted settings.

No matter what setting you are in, it is a challenge to utilize the concepts of a Trust Building Program. It is a juggling act to address the needs of Children Who Hurt and at the same time meet your other obligations.

Group work does not have to detract from or dilute the one-to-one work. On the contrary, it may enhance your work because the trust concepts are presented in a variety of ways.

Trust is still the issue.

Section 4 illustrates how each concept can be adapted. The on-going stories of Shelly, Roger, Tim and Mary are included as illustrative material.

You, the adult, are trustworthy in both settings. Children Who Hurt will recognize that you "preach and teach" the same messages in both settings. This strengthens your relationships. They will be pleased that you try to make everyone feel good. They are glad that you care. It is advisable to tell a Child Who Hurts what you plan to do. "You will hear me talk about commitment, promises, facts, and positive messages with the group. I will not talk about you." Chances are you have been using many of the concepts for years. There is no need to explain to the group about the Trust Building Programs.

Your management of a group and your handling of one-to-one sessions will fit together readily. Each will abet the other.

After a one-to-one program is terminated and the child remains in your group, the use of the now familiar concepts will be reinforcing.

INTRODUCE THE CONCEPTS OF
COMMITMENT AND CONFIDENTIALITY
(Step One)

It is important to start with commitment and confidentiality. Consider a discussion of *friendships*. It is appropriate to say, "I have noticed that some of you seem to be having trouble with your friends. I'll take a few minutes today to talk about friendships. You may wonder, *How come we're going to talk about friendships at the end of a math class?* We have finished our work for today. We have a few minutes to deal with your *social skills*. We use social skills throughout our lives. Learning how to be a good friend is an important social skill."

"Friends must learn about *trust, commitment, and confidentiality.*

"Trust denotes honesty and reliability. It provides feelings of safety and respect.

"A commitment is a promise. It means you will do what you say you will do. It means that you will honor your word—that you can be trusted.

"Confidentiality means being able to keep a secret. It ties in with commitment when someone trusts you with a secret and you say, 'I won't tell anybody.' That's a commitment.

"If you tell, you've broken the agreement. Your commitment wasn't a commitment after all.

"*Happy relationships take hard work.* We are going to deal with how to be a friend so that you will be a happier person."

Teachers no longer need to feel guilty in taking time to provide for the social and emotional growth of the learner.*

Eberle and Hall

MATERIALS AND ACTIVITIES
Friendship Checklist

Group Activity

Purpose: To stimulate thought, discussion, and understanding in interpersonal relationships.

To allow students to discover that individuals have differing feelings about friends and friendship and that friendship is a personal matter.

* Bob Eberle and Rose Emery Hall, *Affective Education Guidebook, Classroom Activities in the Realm of Feelings*, East Aurora, N.Y.: D.O.K. Publishers, Inc., 1975.

Friendship Checklist*

Instructions: If the statement is correct, do not mark it. If the statement is wrong, place an "X" in the space provided.

1. _____A friend is a person who makes you feel good.

2. _____New friends are the best.

3. _____Friends understand you better than others.

4. _____Friends never hurt you.

5. _____True friendships seldom last very long.

6. _____A friend is someone that your parents like.

7. _____Good friends stick up for you even when you are wrong.

8. _____Friends should share secrets.

9. _____To have friends, you need to have money to spend on them.

10. _____To keep friends, you must be honest with them.

Workgroups should consist of four to six students who have marked the *Friendship Checklist*. The teacher will read this list, item-by-item, and discussion will take place within the group. The group will decide, by a vote, which statements are correct.

How to Manage a Friendship (Adapted from *Kids! You Can Manage Your Own Stress*)**

Trust is the basis for friendships. To build trust, you must be honest.

- Tell your friends about your feelings.

- Be sensitive and available for friends. Be a good listener. Don't interrupt.

- If a friend is upset or unhappy, take time to call or visit.

* Bob Eberle and Rose Emery Hall, *Affective Education Guidebook, Classroom Activities in the Realm of Feelings.*
** Ruth Arent and Michelle Waters. *Kids: You Can Manage Your Own Stress!* Denver, Co.: 1982.

- If you have an argument or fight, don't stay mad. Take time to figure out what you did that might have added to the misunderstanding. Peace feels good—work for it.

- Remember, everyone has good days and bad days—especially when you are growing up. Don't let someone else's bad day cause you stress.

- Find a way to be loving, understanding, or supportive. Remember, you have bad days, too, and you don't want your friends to be unkind or nasty.

Have the children choose partners. Discuss each of the How to Manage a Friendship statements. Which are the most important? Are any of these ideas new to you? How would you explain them to your parents?

Together, write a few sentences about trust and promises.

How do people treat each other in a loving way? What do friends *not* do?

Other Projects Students Might Enjoy Have the children write a story about loyalty that tells about friends making up after a misunderstanding, or have them describe what they see as they watch friends greet each other. Do not grade these papers. The purpose of the assignment is to reinforce a focus on friendships, possibly including a special relationship with a brother or sister. Ask the children if this assignment has helped them in any way. If so, how?

Special Considerations for the Child Who Hurts While in the Group Many Children Who Hurt do not have any friends. They are not friendly. They do not risk intimacy. They wish they had friends. That is one reason that they hurt.

This discussion, building from commitment and confidentiality, may give them the important "first steps" needed for them to feel safe enough to venture into a friendship.

The child may consider you the first friend he has ever had, and may welcome the experience of telling secrets, listening, and sharing feelings with a grownup before taking risks with peers.

The Follow-Up in a One-to-One Session

You may want to ask, "In what ways does our relationship resemble a friendship?" or

- "Do you think grownups and kids can be friends?"

- "Do you think counselors and students can be friends?"

- "Do you think parents and kids can be friends?"

- "Do you think teachers and kids can be friends?"

It is acceptable for an adult to enjoy a friendship with a child. A person is a person, regardless of age.

If the child has peer friends, or is starting to make a friend, *encourage the child to tell you good things that are taking place.*

- I'm on time when I go to her house.

- I share my toys.

- I let her choose the TV show.

- We can make plans together. I don't have to be boss.

- I get phone calls. He tells me his secrets.

INTRODUCE THE CONCEPT THAT
LIMITS ARE SAFETY ZONES FOR EVERYONE
(Step Two)

A group is familiar with rules and regulations. It knows there are rules that cannot be changed. Children learn, "This is an okay thing to do," and, "This is *not* an okay thing to do—or way to treat somebody." *Limits promote self-control.* It is reassuring to know that everyone in the group has to obey the same limits. No one feels picked on or discriminated against. Limits can produce a sense of oneness in a group.

Everyone has feelings, and all thoughts and all feelings are understandable. However, *everyone has to limit how they display thoughts and feelings.* Some actions and behaviors are not okay. Some are harmful, to the person or to others. Some are illegal or against the rules. When one cannot express feelings, one may feel frustrated.

Explain that frustrations teach positive messages. They can help to

- build courage and teach self-control.

- promote decisions to choose other ways or activities that are not frustrating—in which success is possible.

- remind the children that *they are okay even if there are people and things they cannot change.*

Materials and Activities   *Coping with Limits and Frustration.* The world abounds in limits. Everyone has to learn to accept frustration as part of life. You may want to hit—but this is not okay. You may want to run away when that's not possible. People frequently react to frustrations by getting angry or feeling helpless.

Frustrations may be large or small, annoying, or very upsetting. Here are some examples. A person may say:

- I feel frustrated when I am telling a story and someone interrupts me.

- I feel frustrated when I start to do my work and the teacher changes the assignment in the middle.

- I feel frustrated when I ask someone to tell me what to do and am told to solve my own problem.

Suggest each person write about a situation or share an incident in which he or she felt frustrated.

These papers are not to be graded. They are to promote increased *understanding* of frustration and the use of limits.

Ask the Children to Describe a Frustrating Situation   What did you do? Was there anything you wanted to do, but you knew it would *not* be appropriate?

Ask the Group   Do you think parents should be strict with their children? If you were a parent, what limits would you set?

Present Selected Items From Activities Pages* for Group Discussion   "Schools have many rules. If you could change any of the rules, which ones would they be and what changes would you make? Why?"

"Parents are not allowed to abuse their kids. It is against the law. What do you think of this law? Do you think that it does any good?"

"Imagine a place where there are *no* limits. What would it be like?"

Special Considerations for the Child Who Hurts While in the Group   A discussion of limits and frustration may be difficult for Children Who Hurt. When others talk of their frustrations, these children may feel some self-pity because their frustrations seem so much more important or difficult.

"I heard Jane say she feels frustrated when she has to wait to play her

---

* The Child Who Hurts may be familiar with these questions. The questions will be new for the others; hence, it will be a new experience for the Child Who Hurts—in listening to what others have to say.

video until her brother finishes his. That's *nothing*. They don't know what frustration *really* is. When my dad screams at me, I want to scream at him. If I did, he'd hit me. That's *real* frustration!"

Take the initiative and repeat to the group:

"All people get frustrated once in a while. When I'm in a hurry, I hate to stop at a red light, but I have to. And when I want to spend money and I can't—when I've reached my limit—that is upsetting, too."

Children Who Hurt seem to be especially interested in information about "spoiled brats." Almost everyone has a little sister, brother, cousin, or neighbor who is spoiled and very bossy. Explain that "spoiled brats" are usually unhappy. They have too much power in the family. They have not had sufficient limits set, and this is scary. They always want to have their own way.

Children Who Hurt have been known to express surprise at this information. "Wow, I thought spoiled brats were *happy* kids." They may think about their own situations where they may feel powerless because a parent is too strict or apt to punish in a harsh way. Talk about moderation. Children want adults to be in control, even if the grownups won't let them do everything they want to do or let them have everything they want to have.

The discussion has merit because Children Who Hurt need to be reminded that there are problems in many, many situations. Parents do the best that they can do.

> **When parents or other adults set limits, it says, "we care."**

The Follow-Up in a One-to-One Session   The child may tell you it is boring to talk about limits. "How about when you give up?" he or she may ask. "That means you've reached your limit," you may answer. The child may also say, "I've tried everything to get my mother to come to a conference and she still won't come. *I give up*" or, "I give up that things at home will *ever* get better," or "I've gone as far as I can go to be nice and friendly, and still no one is nice to me. I give up," or "I can't take it any more." Relate these expressions to the discussion of frustration. Children Who Hurt have a tendency to react to frustrations by feeling defeated and depressed. They need a lot of help to picture that things can get better. They need you to encourage them to try new ways to solve workable problems. They also need help to accept what cannot be changed.

Ask the child to tell you about recent frustrations. Commend the child for reports of self-control and for having a patient, positive attitude.

INTRODUCE THE CONCEPT THAT
DEPENDENCY IS IMPORTANT
(Step Three)

Play or sing the song "People." *"People who need people are the luckiest people in the world."*[1] Translate it into a sad statement—People who *do not* need people may be the *unhappiest* people in the world.

Most people who pretend that they don't need people probably do not trust. They are certain that no one cares—that they have no one to depend on. They do not know how to be a friend or are afraid to try. This unit develops around these concepts. Many do not believe that they are lovable enough to have friends. They think they will always be unlucky. "Unluckiness" is not having a friend.

A person of any age may say, "I can take care of myself. I don't need to depend on anyone." The unspoken thought may be, "But I might be happier if I had a close friend," or, "I would like it if someone would depend on me. I want people to tell me that they care and maybe to tell me that they will protect me if I ever need them."

Materials and Activities Read the following indicators of an unusual need to be dependent.

- constantly needs attention—*"always* bugs me to notice every picture he makes."

- wants to have someone make his or her decisions.

- needs to be close or to touch or hang around.

- needs endless encouragement.

- drops hints or makes demands for miscellaneous gifts, cards, notes.

- asks for help or approval constantly.

- extends invitations of all sorts—"I want you to come and live at my house."

- pretends to be helpless.

Ask the group to add other indicators or cite examples.

Select "needs endless encouragement" for an activity. This can fit in with the discussion on friends.

[1] "People"; Music by Jule Styne, Lyrics by Bob Merrill.

Friends Encourage Friends   Divide the group into partners. State the purpose: to discover many ways to encourage others. Have each couple make up two sentences which mean the same thing as each of the following complete statements.

- "When the going gets tough, the tough get going."

- "If at first you don't succeed, try, try again."

- You have improved in_____.

- You can do_____now that you were never able to do before.

- Everyone makes mistakes. Everyone learns from mistakes. What have you learned from a mistake that you made?

- I believe in you. I like the way you_____.

- I see you have a problem. I know you will work it out. If I can help, please tell me.

- You are a careful planner. You think things through. Sometimes it takes more time, but then it comes out the way you want it to.

Give starter sentences and have each couple discuss how to encourage a person—what they could do if. . . .

- A teacher calls on a shy child. The child starts to cry. . . .

- You're walking in the woods. You have to jump on some rocks to get across a creek. Your friend is scared. . . .

- A friend has to speak at a party for her parents. She is scared. . . .

- A boy has to go to the dentist. He's never been to a dentist before. . . .

All answers are acceptable.

Suggest that students encourage members of the family or neighbors. Urge them to keep aware of how easy it is to be encouraging. Adults should share experiences about an important friendship (spouse, coworker, parent, or other) to show how people depend on each other. Be serious. Be humorous, too. Children must realize that adults need friends, too. *Many families of Chil-*

dren Who Hurt are isolated and suffer from a lack of support from friends and family. Many Children Who Hurt seldom hear encouragement from anyone at home.

> **A sister or brother can be a best friend.**

Select Items From Activities Pages for Group Discussion   "There is a famous quote, *'No man is an island unto himself.'* What do you think it means?

"Do you think it means that everybody needs to be close to someone else?

"What about hermits? Are they happy? Do you believe people can be *too* independent?"

Select other items.

Special Considerations for the Child Who Hurts While in a Group   A discussion about dependency can help friendless children to *picture* the *give and take* of a friendship. From the comments, they may learn what others do not like and get some insight into their own habits. They may understand why others are not friendly and that others have problems, too.

Children Who Hurt may refuse to cooperate in activities or discussions about dependency. By refusing to take part, they display their lack of trust. To talk about depending on others may be too painful. If a child doesn't want to take part, ignore it. On the other hand, a child may say, "I have no one I can depend on," or "Nobody encourages me to do anything. It's as if I don't count," or "Everybody in my family is very independent. I never know when my dad is coming home." Such statements do not require a response from you other than a generic statement such as, "I'm sure that you understand that almost everyone has the need to be dependent on others."

The Follow-Up in a One-to-One Session   If a child has made a poignant statement, discuss it. Embellish with words such as loyalty, understanding, and trust.

Children Who Hurt who come from dysfunctional families are, as you know, loyal to the family regardless of what is going on. They can reveal tunnel-vision thinking: "I've got to be loyal to my mom and dad. I don't have to be loyal to anybody else." They may confide in you that their parents have told them not to get close to others. Unhappy parents teach messages such as "Don't trust anybody. Keep your mouth shut. No one has to know anything about this family. When you get cozy with outsiders, you talk too much. When you keep to yourself, you are safe."

Although a few Children Who Hurt may become clingy, most need to be encouraged to become dependent. It may be the most frightening lesson of all. The path will be irregular and wiggly. At times it will be easier to go backwards. The fact that the children meet with you in one-to-one sessions is a significant breakthrough. It shows that they acknowledge that you care and they are learning to risk some closeness.

INTRODUCE THE CONCEPT THAT
FACTS HELP CHILDREN COPE
(Step Four)

Children sometimes hear facts that they do not understand, or do not want to believe. In many situations, they are curious about these facts but for many reasons do not ask questions. On the elementary level, facts that a counselor or teacher shares are generally undisputed by the class. If Ms. Brown or Mr. Casey said so—so it is! Information from parents may be respected in the same way. If information is contradictory, the children become quite confused.

When children are not told facts, problems arise. They may feel slighted, insulted, disrespected, or afraid. Children who don't know facts tend to imagine unrealistic happenings or blame themselves when things go wrong. Unwarranted blame is harmful.

- Facts are truths. Feelings are real. Feelings can help or hinder how a person accepts or learns facts.

- How you feel is influenced by facts that are told to you. "I was told my parents are getting a divorce. I feel rotten."

- Help children understand that how they learn is influenced by how they feel. "I like math. I do well in math." "I'm unhappy. I don't care what General led that army. I don't want to think about school."

Materials and Activities

Questions for discussion:

1. If someone tells you a secret, this means that you are trusted not to tell. But you break that trust and tell the secret. Your friend finds out. What do you think he or she will say?

2. Someone tells you, "I do not lie. When I talk to you, I tell the truth. I tell you all the facts that I know about the divorce (or Grandma's doll collection or Dad's job). How does that make you feel? Do you agree that someone should tell all the facts they know about a situation?

3. If you don't have the facts about a situation, then you will probably make guesses. For example, parents decide to move to a new house. You are told about it after they have made the decision. They do not explain *why* they decided to move. You guess, "I suppose it's because Mom doesn't like the neighbors." This is not true. The facts are: The new house costs less money. Make up other situations in which someone makes a wrong guess.

Children can cope with almost anything if they are told the facts.

---

4. *Kids like to be told facts but often do not know how to ask for them.* Help children learn to find out what they want to know. Suggest: Please *tell* me. . . . Please *explain* to me. . . . Tell me why we. . . . Give me the *facts* about. . . . Tell me the truth about. . . .

5. Feelings influence how we learn facts. For example, "I feel stupid in science. I don't even try to understand what the teacher explains," or "I feel great today. I'm sure I can pay attention in class and learn these words."

Special Considerations for the Child Who Hurts While in the Group   Facts may be a problem for children with problems. They tend to be *selective* listeners— only attentive to what meets their needs. They tend to be self-focused and only want facts they can use to help them understand their problems. Everything else may be unimportant. "Who cares what the Pilgrims ate. We don't have much food at our house."

These children are impaired memorizers. They do not remember facts that can help them in school or elsewhere. They may resist accepting the relationship between facts and feelings. Some do not recognize or express their feelings. They may be argumentative when you talk about feelings and self-awareness, or appear disinterested in the discussion.

Children Who Hurt may seek facts or details about certain subjects beyond the interest or intensity of others in order to understand their own problems. It is appropriate for you to explain that there must be a limit to some things mentioned in class although in many classes there is considerable discussion of pertinent issues such as divorce, loss, death, feelings, values, prejudice, and so forth. In these discussions, all children can learn worthwhile information that may aid their understanding of their circumstances.

Suggest that the children write down their questions so you can discuss the answers later in private. Tell the children that their questions *are* important to you—you just can't address them in the group setting.

The Follow-Up in a One-to-One Session   A group discussion about facts and feelings may trigger an outburst from a child when you meet next in a one-to-one session. The child may criticize you for leading such a discussion. You may hear, "I don't care what facts other kids want to know about families and problems. *What about me and my family?*" This reflects the natural self-concern of youngsters who have to cope with stressful situations.

The child may say:

- Everybody knows that how you feel about something will determine what you do.

- It's no big deal that everyone has feelings. Kids learn to hide feelings.

- I think Sarah is just putting on a show when she cries like that.

- If kids really tell the facts about what they do or think, they will get in trouble. I think that's dumb advice. It's not for me.

- If feelings affect how you learn facts, and I feel down all the time, I haven't got a chance.

Talk about the child's statements. *Discuss the child's underlying fear or unhappiness or anger.* You may discover that you are the only one with whom he or she can share feelings or ask for facts because you are the only adult the child trusts.

You may be the only adult who is honest with the child.

Sharing facts builds honesty and respect

The group discussion about facts and feelings may provide children with the courage or strength they need to tell you some important information. The children may not be aware of this spin-off.

Emphasize that facts enhance understanding of what is real in their world. This may result in an improved self-image and help children find easier ways to cope with problems.

INTRODUCE THE CONCEPTS OF
STOP! THINK! AND CHOOSE! AND
POSITIVE MESSAGES ARE IMPORTANT
(Steps Five and Six)

The concepts of *Stop! Think! and Choose!* and *Positive Messages Are Important* are basic to providing an understanding that each person is responsible for his or her behavior. The preliminary instructions to the group should be simple. Explain the process: *Stop* doing or saying things you may regret. *Think* before you speak or act. *Choose* to say or do something that will make you feel good about yourself. You may want to talk about impulsiveness and how to control interactions with others. Help children become aware of nice interactions or friendly comments.

Intermittently, in front of the group, commend a child so that the others remain aware that you are aware of how kids treat each other. It reminds the Child Who Hurts that you are *consistent*—that you advocate the same methods in class that you do in one-to-one sessions. At the same time, you demonstrate positive messages.

Materials and Activities Select stories from the Activities Pages. Children offer choices either in discussion or write their answers. Explain the differences between *verbal and nonverbal messages.* After each example that you give, ask, "What else could the person have done?" or "If you were in that situation, what would you say or do?"

Watch videos, TV, films, or filmstrips and analyze the behavior of the characters.

Minidramas or role playing:

Assign characters: Person A—Friendly, Person B—Afraid, Person C—Hostile

Present a situation and have the children act out a response, as per the character.

Situation: Teacher acts mad, stamps her feet, and shakes her finger at a student.

Nonverbal responses:

Person A—*smiles*

Person B—*cries*

Person C—*ignores*

Teacher repeats the motions. Then, children respond with words:

Person A: "Is something the matter? Can I help?"

Person B: "You scare me."

Person C: "Forget it."

Discuss how feelings determine, in part, what you choose to say or do. Instruct the children to make up and act out other situations. Ask, *What do you think of the choices made? What would you say or do?* Also ask, *How do you apologize if there's been a misunderstanding? In what ways?* Discuss solving problems and strengthening relationships. *What does this mean?*

Help children understand that positive messages may include affection, gift giving, and the sharing of personal information, as well as saying and doing nice things for each other. Have the children write short poems or haiku verses picturing positive exchanges. At a later time you may want to list all of the nice interactions described in their writings. Post the list anonymously as a reminder for all.

Special Considerations for the Child Who Hurts While in the Group   Let the Child Who Hurts observe or take part. Listening and observing is learning. This may be the time and place for passive participation. It may be too soon to expect the child to feel confident enough to answer questions or share in class. Perhaps the idea of self-control or impulse control still has little meaning for him. It takes a long time to learn to believe that you choose your behavior. It takes even longer to change from a negative to a positive attitude, as described in *Positive Messages Are Important* (see Page 93).

If you observe the Child Who Hurts managing behavior well, this may or may not be wise to commend in public. Some children are too sensitive and would be embarrassed. Others might misinterpret your praise in public as a violation of what you talk about in private.

The Follow-Up in a One-to-One Session   Class activities and discussion of managing behavior may enrich the work you do in one-to-one sessions. The child may have already talked to you about concepts and is making an effort to put concepts into practice. It is appropriate to acknowledge improvements you have observed as they occur. "You chose to be patient when James held up the line. You used to say, 'Hurry up' or something pushy. Good thinking. Good control!"

Review the notations on the Struggles Charts that you each fill in. Follow the pattern of questions. "What else could you have said or done?" "Were you being good to yourself?" "Was this a loving way to treat someone?"

If the child is still feeling disheartened, ask, "What nice things would you like me to say to you?" Together, develop a list. The items can range from, "You have strong hands," to "You are doing better in math." Ordinarily, compliments will be believable because the child has contributed to the list.

The blending of all concepts becomes complex, and it is unnecessary, indeed, impossible to track the progress of the Child Who Hurts on a daily basis. Inasmuch as there are two trust building one-to-one sessions each week, you may expect that important observations or insights will be revealed and discussed at one time and that others will be evident at another time.

SHELLY REACTS WHEN MISS TIPTON TALKS TO THE CLASS

Shelly does not participate when Miss Tipton shows the class some pictures of faces. Some are happy, sad, and worried. She acts bored. The children's answers identify the emotions.

When Miss Tipton starts talking about being friendly and sharing, loyalty and understanding, Shelly picks up her pencil and starts to scribble. Miss Tipton tells the class a story about her best friend. They had known each other fifteen years. They went to the same school and lived ten houses apart. Once they had a fight—Miss Tipton told one of her friend's secrets. She didn't mean to—it just slipped out. It was a little secret (her friend was planning to call a boy on the phone). If it had been a big secret, it might have been different. Miss Tipton apologized—said she was really sorry. Her friend said it was okay. Miss Tipton wrote her a note, "Dear Nancy, You are my best friend. I'm sorry we had a fight. I was upset that I hurt your feelings. I cried myself to sleep last night. I'll let you borrow my bike anytime you want. Your friend, Betty."

Shelly listens. That afternoon when they meet in private, Shelly asks, "Why did you tell all the kids about your fight with your friend? I don't want them to know about you. Now I know I'm not special to you."

Shelly refuses to hear any explanations. She doesn't care that all kids have to practice being a friend. She wants her teacher to promise not to share any more personal stories with the others.

Miss Tipton will not make such an agreement.

Shelly says, "It's none of their business what you did when you were young or what you like to eat."

Again the teacher insists that she will be as honest with the class as in any other situation.

"Besides," Shelly interrupts, "I didn't even know that your name is Betty. That's my mother's name, too."

ROGER REACTS WHEN MRS. SNYDER TALKS TO THE CLASS

Roger's appointment with Mrs. Snyder follows a class discussion about feelings, in which she had shared her feelings about families. She thinks children should keep in touch with their grandparents. Family loyalty is important. After class, Roger says to Mrs. Snyder, "Why are you talking about the same things with all the kids that you talk about with me? It feels weird to hear you say the same words."

Mrs. Snyder realizes that Roger wants reassurance. He needs to hear that *he is special to her* and he wants her to explain what is going on.

Mrs. Snyder had made a mistake. She had neglected to tell Roger ahead of time that she was going to discuss feelings with the group. She intended to tell him but he was absent the day their appointment was scheduled. It slipped her mind.

Her answers are strong and positive. "Bud, having private sessions with you is important to me. And it is important to me to help all my class understand about feelings and how to make decisions. Every person needs to hear about those things. I hope that when we discuss how to be a friend, everyone will be more friendly to each other. I've noticed more arguing and putdowns in the last week than I've ever heard before."

"Well," Roger says, "It's not boring, but I guess I was afraid you'd tell them about me."

"Oh, Bud—what a silly idea. I wouldn't do that. You should be able to trust me enough by now to know that would never happen. I'm sorry that I didn't tell you ahead of time."

She decides to review Roger's Activities Pages about dependency. "You've never felt you could depend on your mom or dad to understand how you feel or what you want. That's scary and disappointing, I bet." She wants to comfort him but isn't sure of just what to say. She changes the subject. "What kind of a friend are you, Bud? What do you think about the word *loyalty*?"

"When I think of loyalty, I think of soldiers saluting the flag." Roger stands up and salutes the flag that is situated in the corner. "I'd make a pretty good soldier, I think." He starts to parade around the room, standing straight and holding his fingers tight against his brow. "Soldiers are lucky. They get to be away from home. How old do you have to be to go in the Army?"

Mrs. Snyder says, "You're too young, my friend." She gets up, salutes the flag, and parades behind Roger around the desks. They stop in front of her desk and laugh. Roger turns around and spontaneously hugs her legs. He doesn't say anything. She rumples his hair. Their eyes meet for an instant and Roger backs away.

"I'm glad you are my friend. I'm glad you didn't make me talk about my mom and dad."

"I'm not planning to use the word *trust* with the class, Bud. That's reserved for us."

"Thanks," the boy says. "I'm learning about being special." He turns to her—salutes—and walks away with a grin on his face.

TIM REACTS WHEN MR. ATKINS TALKS TO THE CLASS

Tim watches Mr. Atkins put all the volleyball equipment in order for his next class. He doesn't offer to help. Mr. Atkins doesn't ask. It is unusual that Tim doesn't put the balls on the rack and stand on one net-post base while the teacher pulls the other post across the floor.

The boy walks behind his teacher to the office to have a one-to-one session. Both are quiet. Tim looks at his sneakers and fixes the laces which are untied. The teacher waits.

Tim breaks the silence. "I'm mad at you. You told the whole class that you are divorced and you never told me before. I didn't know that you have a six-year-old boy. What's the deal that you would tell them before you tell me?"

Mr. Atkins had discussed living with a single parent with the class. Greg had lost control and pushed Alex over. When Mr. Atkins talked to Greg in front of the group, he asked, "What's bugging you, man?" Greg shouted, "My mom drives me nuts. Ever since my dad left, she's been a 'bossy witch.' Do this. Don't do that. Stop that. Come here. If this is what it's going to be like, I'm ready to move out, but I've got nowhere to go. Some of my friends live alone with their moms but their moms aren't as mean as mine."

"Cool it, Greg," Mr. Atkins had said. "My mom was like that, too, after my dad died. I was nine. Well, she got better. You may have to tough it out for a while but things will get better. As a dad who is alone, I want you to know it is not much fun. I miss my son. He's six and I only get to see him once a month. It costs too much to go to where he lives with his mother. Many kids live with only one parent and they get along fine. Some of the most famous people in the world have lived with a mom or a dad only. Sorry you're not okay with it yet, Greg—but you will be. Kids cope. They get the picture. And just because you're mad at your mom doesn't give you the right to throw your weight around. How about apologizing to Alex?"

After that they chose teams and started the volleyball game.

"Let's clear something up, Tim," Mr. Atkins says when alone with the boy. "I am who I am and I don't plan ahead of time when or what I'm going to tell the class about me. It has nothing to do with our relationship. In here, I know there are issues about relationships and trust that I want to talk about. But don't get bent out of shape because I've never told you that I'm divorced. It's no secret. It's just never come up before."

Tim isn't satisfied. He asks questions about Mr. Atkin's son, Randy, and if Mr. Atkins has a new girlfriend. The teacher tells him that Randy has had a muscle disease since he was a baby. He's a good reader but he has trouble walking. "His mother and I could never agree on how to take care of him. We even went to a counselor to see if we could get along better."

"Well, at least you've told me something you didn't tell the group."

Mr. Atkins ignores the remark. "Kids have got to know that teachers are people, too. My job with you, Tim, is to help you understand that while you are special to me, there are others who need to see the 'human side' of their teachers as well. I teach kids—not volleyball. Get it?"

"Will you ask Greg to come and stay with you?"

"No way, Tim. No way. There are limits that a teacher sets. We've talked about that before. If he were in some kind of a crisis, I'd see him after school and do what I had to do. But there are fifty kids in this school today who are mad at their moms or dads—they'll get over it or work it out. No way am I opening up a *hotel for unhappy kids*."

They smile at each other. Tim wants to know, "Is it easier to be a kid of divorce or a kid whose dad is dead?" Mr. Atkins says he doesn't know. He is philosophical: "All kids, especially teenagers, have something to deal with, Tim. It's not a competition. Even kids who have lots of money and live in fancy houses complain that their parents are never home or they only talk and think about money. One kid told me the other day, 'My dad knows all about the stock market, but he doesn't know my best friend's last name.' " He pauses. "But *no more* of this being jealous of what I tell the class about me. That is not okay.

"Tomorrow I'll read the class some questions from the Activities Pages which we do in here. The other students might like them, and we can have a discussion for a few minutes between halves of the game."

Tim nods his head as if that were okay. "I know you won't tell them about me. I'm sorry I got upset. I guess I needed some kind of reassurance."

The teacher puts his hand on Tim's shoulder. "You've got it, Tim," he says softly.

MARY AND HER FRIENDS
MEET WITH MRS. BRYCE

Mrs. Bryce asks quietly, "Who would like to fill me in on what happened? All of you were sent in here to see me at one time. And it goes without saying that Mrs. Santon was angry. I've never seen her so upset. She's usually a patient and understanding woman. The staff respects her as the principal—a lot."

All six girls stare at Mrs. Bryce. Mary and her five friends are upset. There is no exchange of nervous smiles or any person-to-person communication. It is as if each were in a world of her own.

"I can't stand her," Mary volunteers. "She was mean to us. We were only talking in the restroom, and she smelled cigarettes and blamed us. We were not to blame. It makes me mad to be accused of something we didn't do. And besides, she doesn't trust us to tell the truth and that ticks me off, too."

Mrs. Bryce listens as each girl relates the same story. When she is convinced that they are telling the truth, she goes a step further.

"Would you like to tell me what was so important that you had to hide in the restroom to talk?"

Again, Mary speaks up. The others glance at her. "I know they won't tell you, so I will. Last night we were at Sarah's house. Sarah's brother, Jeff, was drunk and was telling us about the neat ride he and Larry had in a car. They drove it all over town. We know he doesn't have a car so we asked him where they got it. He said, "We borrowed it."

So I asked him, "Who did you borrow it from?"

He screamed at us, "It's none of your business. Keep your mouth shut," and he marched out of the room.

Sarah defends her brother: "It was no big deal. He's 'borrowed' cars before. They were just cruising around. Mary, I think you're jealous cause Larry spends time with Jeff and me and you think he's cute."

Mary doesn't answer Sarah. Instead she expresses her opinion. "I'll bet he stole that car and if he steals once, he'll steal again. Next time, he might get caught and really be in big trouble. Sarah, why don't you tell your mom?"

Before Sarah can answer, Megan gets nasty and says, "Sarah won't tell anybody because she gets to go along sometimes, and being with her brother and Larry *is* a big deal."

Sarah snaps, "Hey, Megan, you wish your brother would pay attention to you. And Mary, if you don't like your brother, that's your problem."

Mrs. Bryce breaks in, "Girls, you're mixing apples and oranges. Borrowing or stealing a car is one issue. Telling on Jeff is another one. If Mary thinks Larry is cute—well, that has nothing to do with what Sarah's brother does. And how family members get along is still something else to think about. Let's try to sort all this out."

She asks Sarah what school her brother attends. Sarah says he quit school a year ago.

"What does he do?"

"He cruises around a lot and sometimes he works at McDonalds."

"Then he has no school counselor to talk to. Sarah, what do you think about telling your parents?"

"My brother would kill me."

Mary speaks up and asks Mrs. Bryce if she can help, and her answer is, "Not without Sarah's permission." Mary volunteers, "Sarah doesn't know about this permission thing which is part of the Confidence Building Program."

Mrs. Bryce explains that she can talk with Sarah and help her Stop! Think! and Choose! what to say or do. All the girls want to know more about how to keep from getting in trouble by not saying or doing something *dumb*. Sarah says she and Jeff are best friends—and always have been. Both parents work two jobs so Sarah and Jeff spend a lot of time together. "I'm not going to 'rat' on him—even if it's true that he stole the car," she admits.

Mary is indignant. "I just think if he stops it now, it will save him from getting in bigger trouble later. Mrs. Bryce, you try to persuade her, won't you?"

"No, Mary. That's not my job. But we can all talk about options, choices, and consequences now if you want to. That might help."

Megan says, "I respect Sarah for being loyal to her brother. Why don't we leave it up to them?"

The group agrees to change the subject and talk about boys. They decide that cute boys get too much attention and that's why they can be hard to get along with. Mary thinks that nobody can get too much attention. She'd like smiles and hugs every day. They all laugh.

Mrs. Bryce quietly brings up the subject of limits at school, emphasizing that the *no smoking* rule is becoming common in many places. It's against the law to smoke on all domestic flights of commercial airplanes, she tells them. The girls repeat that they think it is unfair to be unjustly accused of breaking the rules. The group ends their time together by talking about self-esteem and learning to be assertive.

"We've talked about a lot of things today," Mrs. Bryce says as the girls get ready to leave. "And Sarah, if you want to come in and see me, just let me know."

Mary is the last to leave. As she departs, Mrs. Bryce whispers, "Don't forget your affirmations."

5 ACADEMICS IN A TRUST BUILDING PROGRAM

Teaching is both an art and a science. It combines content and feelings. Every interaction is a lesson. How the learner learns will depend, to a large extent, on his or her emotions. "I hate math," "I'm good at math," and "Math is too hard for me," are meaningful statements. Observe the joy in a child's face when, with hand waving, waiting to be called on, he or she announces for everyone to hear, "I know! I know!"

Children Who Hurt may attend one-to-one sessions and complete a Struggles Chart or the Activities Pages, but if they feel betrayed or shot down by poor grades, it can obliterate the positive effect of the private meetings. Poor grades can negate fleeting feelings of success or the meaning of concepts that you discuss together.

Children Who Hurt may measure school improvement or achievement in concrete terms—i.e., grades. An "F" or a "D" denotes a clear message that "I am no good." *A low grade reinforces the child's familiar low self-esteem. Until students begin to trust that they are really important to you, it is unlikely that academic improvement will become important to them. The trust relationship must preempt academics.*

It is not unusual for Children Who Hurt to tell you that they come to school to meet with you and couldn't care less about classes. Flattering or significant as this may be, your commitment to the student must include a sincere concern for academic improvement and this must be mentioned repeatedly.

> **A person who doubts himself is like a man who would enlist in the ranks of his enemies and bear arms against himself. He makes his failure certain by himself being the first person to be convinced of it.**
>
> **Alexandre Dumas**

Encourage the Child Who Hurts

A Trust Building Program is not a tutorial program, but encouragement is *imperative*. For some children, academic improvement is a benchmark that good things are happening though they may not occur for at least four to six weeks after a Trust Building Program is underway. Overcoming a defeatist attitude is hard work.

With your encouragement, a child can decide to do assignments, and pay attention and participate in class. Happily, a partial success in one endeavor may trigger a willingness to attempt other improvements. Although progress will probably be slow, your commendation is key.

The child may interpret your encouragement as a willingness to help. This may require you to determine:

- What help, if any, with academics should I offer?

- What exceptions should I be willing to accept? Am I willing to monitor the completion of every math problem or written sentence?

- Will I accept late work, sloppy papers, spelling errors, tardies?

- Can I accept inattentive behavior if the Child Who Hurts attempts to and/or completes academic tasks?

- How much, if any, leeway should I permit this student as opposed to others in the class?

- How often will I have to remind this child of important skills to be learned?

Inasmuch as teachers will have only two Trust Building Programs underway at one time, and the students may be in different sections or ask for help in different subjects, their requests may be quite manageable.

Nevertheless, *you decide* on what feels right to you and negotiate a practical program or limits with each child. Given the class situation, try to determine how much teacher attention you will be able to give to the Children Who Hurt. Be liberal at first. *As their confidence grows, the demand for teacher attention will diminish*. Teachers abound in common sense. Your judgment will tell you when to be available to acknowledge every tiny bit of effort and when it is safe to slow down or back off. In some situations, a tutor or student helpers may also be useful.

You are on probation with Children Who Hurt. They want to prove that you don't care—that you, too, are another adult *not* to be trusted. From their point of view, your concern about their academics is one way in which you help them overcome a lack of trust. Help is *accountable*. "My teacher helps me with every math problem. I guess she really likes me." "*My* coach gives *me* extra drill every day. I must be okay."

Modify Teaching Methods

In order to support your commitment to help a child do satisfactory work, you may have to modify your methods of teaching and grading.

The following suggestions are designed to help you work around or sidestep symptoms of hurt that children display, and to promote learning. Among the significant symptoms of anxiety that interfere with academic improvement are an impaired ability to memorize and to concentrate.

Use Methods That Do Not Rely on Memorization   Permit the child to demonstrate skills he or she has acquired by using one or more of the following methods. You may want to offer the same options to all members of the class.

- Offer open-book tests, open-book exercises.

- Offer take-home tests.

- Let the child select answers to be dictated into a tape recorder.

- Let the child create new materials that show an understanding of concepts. The materials will depend on notes or texts—not content that needs to be memorized.

- Let the child teach concepts to others using text or handouts that you have provided. This can be especially helpful in developing trust and self-esteem.

- Promote cooperative testing or cooperative development of displays or materials which demonstrate or clarify concepts.

- Organize dramatizations of materials with readings from scripts. This can also be helpful in developing self-esteem.

- Let the child explain displays or experiments, pictures or documents to the group or to you.

- Have the child hand in completed contracts.

Find Ways to Help a Child Learn to Concentrate

- Check for distractions—too much noise, too many art displays, or confusing mobiles.

- Monitor placement of child's desk or table. Is it too close to other students who are inattentive, hyperactive, or acting inappropriately?

- Take the initiative in one-to-one sessions to discuss problems or feelings that you recognize as interfering with the child's ability to concentrate. Problem solving can relieve the stress that can block learning.

A child may be able to visualize the completion of small assignments and focus on getting finished. Having too much work can be perceived as overwhelming. The child's attention spins off before he or she may even make any attempt to start. Make sure that assignments are manageable.

Guard Against Unnecessary Competition

- Provide activities wherein each child becomes aware of his or her own strengths and weaknesses. Emphasize that each person has a "mix-and-match" bundle of abilities, and one is not better than the other, only different. A star athlete may not be a painter, for example. The class president may be terrified of a snake. A cautious reader may tell the funniest jokes.

- In elementary school, arrange displays on bulletin boards in alphabetical order—A's and B's this week, C's and D's next week, and so forth.

- Don't permit children to choose teams if you anticipate that some will always be selected last. Oftentimes, the poorly coordinated or hesitant contributor is impaired because of problems—personal or family problems. *Why add hurt to the child who already hurts?*

Help the Child Learn to Organize. Disorganization reflects an inability to get focused or stay focused. Provide lists or outlines whenever possible. A disorganized person cannot anticipate a step-by-step progression and final product, answer or result. Children Who Hurt—who live in chaos—are disorganized because they tend to *disbelieve* that things happen in an orderly way or that it is possible to predict any future outcome. They frequently dread the future and are predictably pessimistic and depressed.

> Academic lessons, governed by facts and procedures, often become solemn lectures punctuated with pauses for questions. Unwittingly, classes are, as Charles Silberman discovered, "grim, joyless places." Children Who Hurt live in grim, joyless places. The classroom must be different. In the class, the child must find release from worry and despair *and* evidence that schoolwork has been learned. Hopefully, this will begin a progression from negativity to optimism.[1]

Provide Numerous Experiences in Decision Making. Jim Fay, in *Tickets to Success*,[2] shares concern that we need to help children understand decision making. Furthermore, we need to give them opportunities to make good decisions *and even allow them to experience ones that they will regret*—while showing empathy and following through with the consequences. He wants them to learn to ask, "How is this going to affect me?"

I want children to have so many opportunities to make decisions when they are little and to feel consequences—that by the time they get to making life and death decisions, they have had so much practice they automatically ask themselves, "How is this going to affect me?"

Share Stories About Yourself Again and Again. Let children know you as a model of maturity and understanding.

Offer Contract Learning as an Option Contracts are designed to help overcome distraction, disorganization, and discouragement. Not a single contract, but an ongoing array of contracts add up to academic improvement and improved self-esteem.

A contract represents an achievable, short-range goal. It is usable at any grade level. The technique is to put into contract form the skills or content objectives (or data from a pretest) that the student needs to work on. Adjustments should be made to meet any special learning needs. (See details, Page 193.)

Use the Pretest/Post-test Method as a Teaching Technique. The pretest includes skills that most students have mastered. At the same time, it introduces new information, tasks, or skills that are to be mastered. Thus, it becomes a presentation of facts; the specifics of what lies ahead. When the child knows what is ahead, he or she is less fearful than when presented with entirely unfamiliar lessons or assignments. (See details for procedures, Appendix Page 196.)

---

[1] Chas. E. Silberman, *Crisis in the Classroom*, N.Y.: Vintage Books, 1971.
[2] Jim Fay, *Tickets to Success*, 2207 Jackson St., Golden, CO 80401, Cline/Fay Institute, 1988.

> Test taking can be the ultimate moment of fear. For Children
> Who Hurt, it may be tantamount to panic. Anxiety runs wild.

Use Test Items as Teaching Materials to Help Children Who Hurt Experience Improvement in Academics The teacher should present test items or problems for explanation, drill, or mastery. When the children are presented with the test then, the questions should feel familiar and anxiety is diminished, if not eliminated. The purpose of tests is to measure what the children have learned, not to scare them so that they cannot perform well.

All teaching methods are intended to improve the damaged self-esteem of Children Who Hurt. Educators hope that students will become successful test takers, but that is but one of their goals. Test taking must be considered among the skills that teachers teach.

Teaching to the test does not invalidate what is learned.

Grades and Reports

Grades are a disturbing issue for many teachers as well as children. District policies may be rigid. There may be few, if any, options to provide much-needed encouragement for children who are beginning to make an effort to do better. Discuss this with the Children Who Hurt in one-to-one sessions. You can commend improvements. In some instances, you can report "Work in Progress" to prevent poor interim grades that may be discouraging.

What about grades that the student receives from other teachers? This may be a serious problem if the student continues to undermine his chances of success by refusing to attend, behave, or produce. *Do not overreact or feel that your work is to no avail because no improvement has occurred in some classes.* Stay focused on your Trust Building Program—how the student works with *you*. If you are a counselor, you and the student should select at least one class or one teacher to whom you can suggest contract learning or the other modifications described in this chapter.

Once a student experiences a series of successes such as completed contracts with acceptable grades, his or her confidence will begin to grow. *Confidence motivates learners to learn.*

The spin-off from the Trust Building Program into academics can affect the home situation. When a student brings home a report which notes an improved attitude about learning and improved grades, these are important messages to parents. The improvements may result in a decrease in tensions between parent and student. The decreased tensions, in turn, can further benefit academic performance.

Teacher Strategies for One-to-One Sessions

Purpose: To foster a positive attitude toward school. To convince the Child Who Hurts that one responsibility of the adult in a Trust Building Program is to support the child's efforts to improve academic work.

Directions: Talk about what you and the student can do to reduce student anxiety and initiate changes with various teachers. Express these ideas in your style. Use your own vocabulary.

Important Teacher Statements to Express to a Child

- In order for you to feel good about yourself, you have to see that you are accomplishing things in school. This means that you have to do assignments and take tests. Don't be discouraged by disappointing grades. You can always improve. You may have some weaknesses that need attention.

- I understand that you may have trouble concentrating and memorizing.

- You can decide to do your work even if you do not like your teacher.

Consider some of these ideas on how you may possibly work with your teachers to improve your work or get the help that you want.

- The more you tell your teachers about *how* you learn, the greater the chance that they will make some adjustments or changes to help you. For example, do you prefer to read aloud or write things rather than just listen? Teachers want kids to learn. That's why they are teachers.

- Teachers have to follow rules just like kids do. Often the rules have to do with grading. *Ask your teacher to consider ways to grade you for improvement, effort, and attitude* even if you still have skills to learn or work that you haven't completed. Perhaps an "Incomplete but catching up" can be reported or "Work in Progress."

- Ask if you can grade yourself or agree on a grade ahead of time as you start a project or negotiate a contract.

- If you have had a problem getting to school or paying attention, it is understandable that you may be behind in your work. You cannot catch up on all your work at the same time. We can work out a plan so that you will not try too much too fast, or too soon. You can share this plan with your other teachers.

Even though we are in a Trust Building Program, *I cannot be your tutor.* I can encourage you and praise you. You are the one who must decide to do your work and ask for help when you need it. When you are in my class, I will help you as I do the others.

- Offer to confer with other teachers regarding the suggested modifications described above.

- Introduce relaxation exercises or stress management techniques if the child is tense.

- Suggest diversions such as entertaining books to read, videos to watch, or computer games to play—to encourage levity or change of pace.

Promote Discussion

Select items from the Academic Activity Page.

End of the Session

Set the time for the next one-to-one session.

End with an optimistic personal statement such as, "I'm looking forward to seeing you again. I'm sure we can. . . ."

Use affirmations. Repeat instructions as often as necessary.

The single most important factor motivating students is encouragement. Skill in encouraging is a prerequisite for effective teaching.[3]

Jon Carlson and Casey Thorpe

MISS TIPTON TALKS TO SHELLY ABOUT SCHOOL WORK

Shelly uses the markers to decorate her nails. She doesn't put the tops back on. She refuses to look up when Miss Tipton asks for attention. It is obvious she is in a bad mood, and at the same time, looks spacy.

It is time for the children to follow directions and draw a picture of four

[3] Jon Carlson and Casey Thorpe, *The Growing Teacher* (Englewood Cliffs, N.J.: Prentice Hall, 1984).

(Continued on page 154)

ACADEMIC IMPROVEMENT

Directions: Read the questions. Fill in the blanks.

Reminders:
There are no right or wrong answers.
Handwriting and spelling don't count.
All answers are confidential.

One reason for a Trust Building Program is to encourage you to do your best and to feel good about your improvements and successes.

Let's look at how *you take care of yourself* in the classroom. Most teachers urge students to ask the questions that they need to ask. If you do not understand what the teacher has explained, what do you do?

_____

_____

You have to turn in your papers when the bell rings. If you are not pleased with what you have done or feel it is not finished, what do you do?

_____

_____

_____

If you need help with your work, what do you do? _____

_____

_____

When a teacher gives an assignment, make an agreement with your teacher about how long you have to finish. Each person learns at a different pace (or rate). You do not have to be a fast learner to be a good learner.
Tell your teacher how *you* learn.
Fill in these sentences. They will help you to talk to your teacher.

It is easy for me to _____

_____

It is hard for me to _____

_____

Academic Activity 1-1, continued

I get stuck when _____

_____

_____

If I get stuck, I need help to _____

_____

_____

I have to read something before I can remember it. _____

_____

When I hear something, I can learn it better _____

_____

When I want to memorize something, I write it down over and over again. The writing helps me to remember _____

_____

Many boys or girls get upset or distracted if others are talking or walking around. Are you a person who needs to be alone or needs to be where it is quiet? If so, how would you tell your teacher so she might arrange for you to go to a quiet place?

I study best when _____

_____

_____

I need to be alone _____

_____

Grades can be unfair. Some children know a lot about certain things like caring for animals but cannot do well on a math test. When they fail math, they feel bad. *Ask for all the help you need.* Be proud of your efforts.

Some teachers give grades only from test scores or paper work. This does not encourage kids who are trying hard and beginning to improve. That seems unfair. If this happened to you, what would you do?

_____

_____

If you get a grade on a paper or a test that you think is unfair, what would you do?

_____

_____

_____

_____

152

There are many ways to show your teachers that you have learned what you have been taught. Which of these ways are your favorites?

Write a paper telling about what you have learned. _____

Take a test. _____

Teach what you have learned to another person. _____

Tell the teacher or record in a tape recorder. _____

Academic activities:

Make up a test or make some pictures, charts, sentences, spelling lists, and so forth.

Put on a play or act out a scene using what you have learned about.

Make a diorama or a costume.

Write some poetry, stories, or articles using words you have learned or other interesting information.

When kids are upset, they cannot do their best work. It is best to tell your teachers when you are upset. What do you think about the following statement in the box below?

> I can still see the hatred on my dad's face. That expression—his feelings—were real.
> I read them!
> I memorized them!
> But that same day, I couldn't answer all the questions on my history test.

balls and four animals. Shelly continues to paint her nails. When the other children start their work, Miss Tipton approaches Shelly quietly.

"In first grade we learn to follow directions. We learn study habits to use for many, many years. I'd like to see you draw the balls and the animals. Which animals do you like best?"

Shelly doesn't look up. She makes no eye-to-eye contact. "I don't like animals. I hate everything and I'm not coming to our special meetings any-more."

Miss Tipton wants to encourage the child. "I look forward to talking with you, Shelly. I will see you when the bell rings, as planned. Meanwhile, if you don't want to draw animals, you can select four animal stamps and ar-range them on your paper." Shelly takes four stamps and tears them up.

When they meet together, the teacher asks her to share what is upset-ting her. She says, "I got my paper back with the three clouds. It said 'O.K'. Mary got *her* paper back with three clouds and she got a smiley-teacher sticker and I didn't. You are an unfair teacher. You like the other kids better than you like me."

Miss Tipton is aware that the Trust Building Program is being tested. At the same time, she decides to talk about assignments and classroom work.

"Something puzzles me, Shelly. You use big words. You understand complicated stories and ask wonderful questions. You are a fine thinker. Why do you refuse to do the work you are asked to do?"

With a shy glance at her teacher, Shelly explains, "It's too easy. I wish you'd let me do what I want to do. I'd like to make up some stories and tell them to the kids or I'd like to twirl and dance to music. Do you remember when I twirled for you one time? You said you liked it."

"Maybe you would like harder work to do, but in school we have to follow instructions just like I have to stop at a red light when I drive my car. I'd like to help you develop good study habits now. I also will make certain that you have time to do creative things that talented girls love to do. Do you put up a fuss when your grandmother asks you to do things?"

Shelly doesn't answer. She picks up the markers and draws—then stops. Shelly adds one more reason why she doesn't do her work: "I'm afraid to make a mistake. I hate myself when I do something wrong or I'm not as good as the other kids."

Miss Tipton takes time to explain about smart, gifted learners. "Many hate to follow instructions. They are perfectionists, yet they want to be crea-tive. They often have trouble with grownups. None of your complaints are unusual, Shelly, and I know they bother you a lot. We'll work on each com-plaint. I want you to like school."

Miss Tipton and the girl come up with a plan. Shelly will follow instruc-tions and finish her work as soon as possible without rushing, and then she can do something creative—no extra work just because she finishes more quickly than others. Shelly will evaluate her own work, keep track of her papers, and together they will decide on the comments for her report card.

Shelly will find ways to compliment the good work of other classmates without feeling jealous or put down. If she can say, "I think your picture is pretty" the other children might be more friendly and Shelly may be happier at school.

Miss Tipton reminds Shelly to use affirmations. "Shelly, let's hear you say, 'I am a nice person. I deserve friends.' " Shelly repeats this three times. Then she says, "But sometimes I'm not nice and I'm sorry I said you were an unfair teacher. I deserve to let myself make mistakes." She has a soft expression on her face as she goes to greet her grandmother who waits at the door.

MRS. SNYDER TALKS TO ROGER ABOUT SCHOOL WORK

Roger has an assignment to write a book report. He read a book about racing cars and enjoyed it. He wants to tell about the story and the pictures. He read the book all by himself. He had settled behind some shelves in a privacy corner and read it out loud quietly. Reading out loud has been the new agreed upon plan. He has concentrated well—a marked improvement.

Now Roger wants to try a written book report. He has a good idea what Mrs. Snyder wants but he thinks he had better ask. One question, "Mrs. Snyder, do I have to tell about how Jerry got interested in cars?" is followed by another question, a third, a fourth, and so on.

Mrs. Snyder is concerned. *How can I set limits now and still keep this boy's new-found excitement and willingness to work?* She decides to ask him to limit his questions to just five or six.

By the time Roger's report is finished, Mrs. Snyder is weary but delighted. Roger has had an important taste of success. Mrs. Snyder suggests that he take the report home and show it to his parents. He doesn't say anything. A few minutes later she watches Roger put the report in the basket. He is still convinced that no one cares. After school, Mrs. Snyder rescues the paper and slips it into her desk. "I've got a lot of work to do with this boy," she muses.

As part of every day, Mrs. Snyder permits Roger to choose what he wants to work on. Today when he hands in his papers, he tells her, "I don't get so mad anymore. I hate it when grownups tell me what I have to do. It's like they only notice me when they have to give me orders. I'm glad you're not so bossy."

"I'm glad we figured out a way for you to like to do your work, Bud. Good job." Roger smiles.

Roger starts to wander around the room. He decides he wants to watch a film strip on monkeys, but he can't find it. He looks at a display of butterflies but that doesn't interest him. He goes back to his table and pouts. He doesn't pick up his library book or take out his crayons to pass the time until his Trust Building Session with Mrs. Snyder. No one pays any attention to his pout. No one pays any attention at all.

In the one-to-one session with Mrs. Snyder, he is sullen. "I'm glad we can be together, Bud. Why the frown? Just a few minutes ago you were smiling." He has a list of complaints. "I didn't get to use the computer. I couldn't find the filmstrip that I wanted. You never let me do a report with Vernon and he's the only friend I've got. I hate math. I don't get to write on the board as much as I want to."

Mrs. Snyder looks skeptical. "What's *really* bugging you, Bud?"

"I'll tell you," Roger begins. "Report cards come out next week and I'm afraid my parents will get mad again. They do look at my report card and tell me I can do better. Dad says he didn't like school but still he asks me, 'Are you dumb, kid? or do you have to be grounded for a few weeks so you can do better?' I think that's a stupid question. They never take me anywhere so what's to be grounded about?"

Mrs. Snyder decides to talk about grades and report cards. She reads over the Activities Page about different ways that students can show teachers what they have learned. Roger admits that Mrs. Snyder already lets him do a variety of things. "But my other teachers make me take tests. I'd really like it if Mr. Shaw and Ms. Upton would give me a 'Work in Progress. Trying Hard'— I'd feel better."

His teacher urges him to talk to them. At the end of the session, Mrs. Snyder mentions the affirmations.

"I am entitled to talk to my teachers about my grades."

"I deserve to get a grade that tells my parents that I am working hard at school."

"Bud, don't get discouraged," his teacher says. "It takes a lot of hard work to raise a grade from one level to another. You feel as if you'll never catch up or do better, but you will. In my class, your contracts aren't finished yet and I'm sure you'll do well. Next time you can ask Vernon if he will work with you. Vernon has been doing some extra work in math because he was absent when he was sick. He might be glad to start a Social Studies contract with you. I've noticed that he sits next to you at lunch and you two guys seem to be good friends."

Roger twists his mouth as he answers, "Since you've been my friend, I like school better and maybe that's why I can be more friendly to the kids."

"I'm glad, Bud," she says as she helps him put on his jacket.

MR. ATKINS TALKS TO TIM ABOUT SCHOOL WORK

"I have a headache," Tim announces as he walks into Mr. Atkin's office. "I think it's because my eyes hurt and there are too many people in my English class. It's so noisy in there that nobody gets anything done."

"How can I encourage you today?" Mr. Atkins asks.

"I can't figure out what Mr. Springer wants me to do," Tim complains. "He breaks us up into groups. I'm in with six other kids. I didn't like what one of the kids suggested and I said so. Next thing I know, Mr. Springer tells me to go and work by myself. I get the picture that he doesn't think I have anything to contribute. When I'm off by myself, he says 'Some day you'll learn to cooperate in a group' and walks off."

"We're talking about different things, Tim. Maybe you don't understand how to fit in when a teacher sets up a cooperative learning pattern or maybe Mr. Springer simply thought you might be happier by yourself."

"Then why didn't he ask?"

The boy and Mr. Atkins discuss ways teachers try to meet the needs of their students. Mr. Atkins uses the word "individualized" and explains about cooperative learning. Tim understands that kids interact together in order to do a project and that everyone is important. He admits that when he was so critical that he was not helping the group to figure out what to do and how to do it.

"I know you're upset when you tell me you are overwhelmed or feeling critical. Maybe you're over-tired, too."

Tim tells Mr. Atkins, "Last night I stayed up watching a late movie—alone. No one cares what time I go to bed or if I have nightmares—and I did. So I am tired. Maybe Mr. Springer figured out that I needed time alone. I did finish my work when I worked alone." Then he adds, "I'll try to get along better with the kids, too."

Group arrangements, privacy, and cooperative learning are concepts Tim understands. He promises to look at the Activities Pages tonight.

Mr. Atkins makes one further suggestion. "When your eyes get tired, Tim, ask your teacher if there is someone who can read the paragraphs to you so you can learn with your ears. That's what kids can do if they need to—they learn to *compensate*. The ears can take over for the eyes in order to help out."

"I'll try it," he says.

Together they discuss that when you criticize others, you may be showing that you feel critical of yourself. "Sounds complicated to me," Tim says, "but I get it." He then says, "If I can finish three more assignments in that class, I'll get a 'C' and that'll be great. I've never had a 'C' in English before."

"I'm proud of you, Tim."

Before it is time for Tim to leave, he states his affirmations and repeats three times, "I'm capable of learning. I can get okay grades."

"Say it again and again, Tim. It's music to my ears," Mr. Atkins says.

MRS. BRYCE TALKS TO MARY
ABOUT SCHOOL WORK

Mrs. Bryce has a notice on her desk that Mary is failing in Science. As her counselor, she is required to call Mary into the office. She does not want to confuse this meeting with their Confidence Building Program session scheduled for the next day. At the same time, here is an opportunity for Mary to see that academic success *is* an integral part of a Confidence Building Program.

Some of the complaints that Mary brings up about her Science class do not seem unreasonable. The teacher, Mr. Ryan, and Mary have had a series of run-ins and misunderstandings since the semester began. He is a strict teacher who wants the students to learn a lot and becomes agitated when one of the students is inattentive or disrespectful. Mary, as an attention-getter, will deliberately do or say things to upset him and then accuse him of being an unfair grouch.

When Mary sees the notice, she acts as if it were unimportant. "I've never gotten an 'F' before—darn that man anyhow! I *suppose* I have to do something about it," she adds dejectedly.

"I suppose you do," Mrs. Bryce concurs, and they proceed to develop a plan to find out what work needs to be completed and how.

"I asked you once to get me out of his class and you wouldn't do it. Will you do it now?"

"No way, Mary. In the first place, there is no other Science class that fits your schedule, and if you're going to be a nurse, you'll have to work with a lot of people who are rigid and demanding. Look at Mr. Ryan as example Number One. You'll have to find a way to get along with him."

"You're no help, Mrs. Bryce." She picks up the notes they had written and leaves.

The next day at their Confidence Building Session, Mrs. Bryce greets Mary in her usual warm way. She hands her the Activities Pages relative to academic success. She decides to look over the items with Mary rather than bring up the subject of Mr. Ryan and Science class.

Mrs. Bryce interrupts what they are doing and says, "Mary, have you forgotten that you are important to me and that I want you to feel good about yourself? Part of feeling good about yourself is doing well in your classes. You want to be a nurse—that's great. Let's work toward that goal. If you're mad at Ms. O'Brien, Mr. Ryan, or Mr. Brown, come and tell me. Your friends will still be your friends even if you decide to get along with your teachers. You're taking care of yourself if you bring up your grades and that's what counts."

"But suppose I still hate Ms. O'Brien and Mr. Ryan?"

Mrs. Bryce avoids the question. "I had a teacher in college who was dull—I mean *boring*. I'd fall asleep every day. Then I got a failing notice and I decided in a hurry that he knew his subject and I didn't, so I'd better get my act together. It didn't matter that he had the personality of a flat pancake. I'd be the one who would fail. I can't help it if Ms. O'Brien doesn't smile in class or that Mr. Ryan is critical and sarcastic. That's just how it is. The rest is up to you."

Mary goes on to tell about how her brothers and sisters always put her down. She's sick of it.

"You are learning to build your self-esteem, Mary. Let's continue with affirmations."

As Mary departs from the session, she repeats, "I have a good brain. I can be successful in my classes and still have my friends."

6 WHEN THE CHILD TESTS A TRUST BUILDING PROGRAM

WHEN THE CHILD WHO HURTS ACTS OUT IN A GROUP

Learning to trust is a gradual process, always in flux. Children will test the program—thereby testing you. Two common tests are: *losing control in a group*, and *befriending a group troublemaker*—a child who is disrespectful to you.

A Crisis in the Classroom Some kids may drive you up the wall occasionally. Some are famous for being difficult. The Child Who Hurts, with whom you meet one-to-one, may fall apart. A crisis is an unwelcome event. Your management of the group or an individual should parallel your management of one-to-one sessions as best you can. This is not an easy task.

It is, however, predictable. Your Child Who Hurts will fall apart at some time. Chances are it will happen within the group. Efforts to learn control, think positively—even in practicing the habit of using a pleasant tone of voice are sporadic. The ten, twelve, or fourteen one-to-one sessions will indeed have impact, but slippage there will be. It is not your fault. Don't personalize it. *It does not signal that your Trust Building Program has been a failure.*

Handling the Episode You meet with Jim on a regular basis. He is beginning to open up to you. But he is still a first-class tease. He has mastered the art of grabbing someone's books and darting around the room so the other child can't get them back. Occasionally, he throws in a few obscenities to make things more colorful. You ask him to stop and give back the books. You are ignored. Other children get in the act. Some cheer him on. It is *chaotic*.

What do you do? You handle Jim the same way you always have. If there are consequences to be carried out—so be it. *Just because a child is in a Trust Building Program does not mean that he or she is free to act out.* Inasmuch as no one else may even know about the one-to-one sessions, it would be inconceivable to see Jim lose control and let him get away with it.

Address Jim in Front of the Group.   "Jim, disrupting this class is not okay. If you're upset about something, there are lots of other ways to show it. If you need time out, you know where to go."

There are to be no special considerations for this child. The standards of behavior that you expect should be the same for everyone.

Bear in mind that this behavior is a symptom of hurt. It reaffirms one reason the child was selected for a Trust Building Program in the first place.

Follow-up in the One-To-One Session.   Begin with the usual protocol. Start with a welcoming statement: "I'm glad we can meet together. It seems as if this is a good time to see what's happening. Obviously, something upset you today. If you were angry or disappointed, say so. Your feelings count, too." *Caution:* Don't rehash the crisis or acting-out episode if the matter has already been handled with appropriate consequences. Initiate a discussion of what precipitated the incident—that's what's important.

If you remain calm, you may want to explain your calmness. The child may need to hear you say, "I have learned to appear calm in a crisis. Because I am calm does *not* mean that I don't have feelings or that I don't care for you or that I will not become involved." This may be dramatically different from how mother or father reacts when the child misbehaves at home. The child may be accustomed to hysterical outbursts mixed generously with threats. His rage at home may be matched by someone else's fury.

If he asks you, "Don't you *ever* get mad?" that's a fair question from his point of view.

"Of course I do. You know that. But is it necessary for me to get angry at you to prove that I like you? Is it important to you to test our relationship to make sure that I mean what I say? If it is—that's okay—but let's talk about it. Let's find other ways for you to check me out without teasing someone and disturbing the class."

Expect denial. "Our meeting together has nothing to do with taking Greg's books. He's been wising off to me and I got mad."

This may be accurate. It may have only been a display of Jim's impulsiveness.

Don't debate.

You may reassure the Child Who Hurts, "I've worked with other boys and girls, and I know that it's hard to control yourself all of the time. You've been doing such a good job. You can go right back to doing a good job."

- You may want to help him or her verbalize the Stop! Think! and Choose! options that he could have selected.

- If the child feels discouraged or guilty, read over improvements the student has made that you've collected in the Struggles Charts. These positive reminders are important for you, too.

Choosing an Undesirable Friend   A Child Who Hurts may develop a friendship with a kid who is disruptive or rude to you. Even if, in your estimation, it is the "wrong kid" or a member of a "wrong gang," *this may be the first friend the Child Who Hurts has ever had.*

This is a puzzling situation. Did the child deliberately seek out the wrong kid—the trouble maker—in order to test you or were there other reasons? Was the child drawn into this relationship because he/she is vulnerable, a "follower," or being set up in some way? Is the child now too "grateful" for the attention from the other(s) and unconcerned about your feelings? In most cases, it just signals that peer acceptance is more powerful than the developing trust relationship with you. The child is not rejecting you.

You cannot select friends for someone else. You can discuss, with the child, the possible problems that may arise because the friend's rudeness indicates deeper concerns. The two friends together may get into trouble or lose interest in school. Children Who Hurt are usually immature and don't think about what might happen in the future. The excitement of having a friend preempts everything else.

Be realistic. It is questionable that anything you say will change the relationship between the two kids. Discuss friendships if you choose but don't expect the Child Who Hurts to give up a friend. That's asking for a cognitive decision that conflicts with strong emotions. When the friend is unpleasant to you, focus on his or her problems. Detach this from the Child Who Hurts and the trust you have been working to establish.

The child's recovery is your mission. That may be as far as it goes. Fondness for you is not the issue. New peer friendships may be heralded as a sign that the child has learned about relationships—even though you receive minimal positive feedback.

A Trust Building Program is not a popularity contest. The child may not like you because of old attitudes toward adults but will still come to the one-to-one sessions. If attendance becomes irregular because of the influence of the "wrong kid," confront the matter. The Child Who Hurts may have to resolve that it's okay to remain friends with someone who doesn't respect you and still come to one-to-one meetings.

> **Don't even consider it! Don't drop a Trust Building Program because the Child Who Hurts joins a group of unmotivated kids or makes friends with a peer who has problems of his own. Peer acceptance is powerful. A Trust Building Program may not be powerful in quite the same way.**

Reminders for Adults Don't get discouraged when Johnny is just Johnny— acting like a clown, being a wise guy, or attempting to drive you crazy. His zest for life is refreshing even if difficult to manage.

You haven't failed as a disciplinarian or as his friend. Johnny is just being Johnny, and he is more controlled than he used to be.

Don't fret if today you got angry with Johnny and yesterday you were patient. Celebrate! You're human. You are a person with feelings.

7 MESSAGES TO PARENTS: A SPECIAL ART, A NECESSARY TASK

A Trust Building Program is not designed for parent participation. Nevertheless, most parents will be aware of the one-to-one meetings either because they signed a permission slip, you informed them in another way, or the child talks about them. Accordingly, all messages to parents become a special art as well as a necessary task.

Children who do not trust become manipulators. When they misrepresent what goes on—exaggerate, distort, or minimize—they manage to keep adults in turmoil. Parents may not understand at all what is going on at school. Counselors and teachers may be equally confused by the reports about what goes on at home. Kids may derive some sort of satisfaction from the disharmony between their parents and the school. They observe that the adults involved become uncertain how to relate to each other or that they become openly hostile and confronting. Such repercussions appear to reaffirm for some children that adults are not to be trusted. They seem to thrive on this disharmony. They do not realize that such disharmony increases their own feelings of anxiety and insecurity. This may result in further inappropriate behavior. They manage to manipulate the adults into a pattern of misunderstanding, misrepresentation, and mutual mistrust. This may inadvertently reinforce the belief that their own feelings of mistrust are justified.

From the point of view of the counselor or teacher, this is an untenable situation. As an adult, you do not have to be victimized by the manipulations of a child who has never learned to trust. *You must establish a clear feedback system to the child's parents even though you may be greeted with disdain, hostility, or indifference. The child must witness your strength on his or her behalf.* It can override any messages he or she brings home. The child can witness that the adults in his or her world do care.

> **The success of a trust building program depends on you. Trust builds between you and the Child Who Hurts.**

Parents need the reassurance that your work with their child is designed to encourage children and build their self-esteem. It is to inspire children to trust that you are committed to their happiness, success, and improvements in behavior and/or attitude. You will stay child-focused. If children share something about life at home, you will help the children understand their own behavior and what they can and cannot do.

Do not be critical of parents.

Be certain to state that a Trust Building Program is only one of many ways that school professionals, mentors, or youth leaders reach out to children.

GUIDELINES FOR PARENTS

These statements are intended to allay parental anxiety about the child or the invasion of family privacy.

- There will be no reports about what the child shares. The program is built on *confidentiality*.

- The parent is *not* invited to attend sessions.

- There is no way to determine exactly *how many* sessions there will be. You propose 14 to 20 short meetings—some may be as short as two minutes.

- Regardless of what the child reveals, the adult will focus on the child's reactions, feelings, and behaviors. The child will be helped to change his or her behavior and to solve problems.

- Some of the sessions will deal with self-control, positive communication, the expression of feelings, and self-acceptance.

- There may not be any observable changes in behavior at home.

- There may or may not be improvement in academics. Improvements may be spotty and inconsistent.

- The parent is asked *not* to request progress reports. Parents will be informed of some improvements, as they are noted, by a telephone call or written note with the child's knowledge.

- Sometimes there may be phone calls between the child and the adult. These calls are important because they convey the message to your child that, "I am important to my counselor (teacher)—both in school or out of school." Calls may be scheduled in lieu of a face-to-face meeting.

- Lastly, your child is special. I want this to be the most successful year he or she has ever had at school. This is the same message I have told your child.

These statements strengthen your position as a caring professional, and show your awareness that emotions can interfere with learning and cause kids to behave in ways that alienate others. You show that you are willing to take time to help the kids who need your help.

It is not your responsibility to become involved in the parent-child relationship.

POSSIBLE PARENTAL RESPONSES

The Disinterested Parent It is best that you do not anticipate parental enthusiasm. Some parents will be supportive and others will be disinterested in your plan. Many parents of Children Who Hurt are stressed out, bewildered, or worried about the family and the children. Others may not derive pleasure from parenting. Some are casual or unconcerned about how their child is doing in school. They do not concern themselves with self-esteem or motivation.

If the parents are disinterested, it is not a repudiation of you or an implication that the parent is not a loving parent. It may be just a point of view. "My kid is just a kid. He'll grow out of it. He's not a big problem at home. Do what you need to do to get him to do better at school." The "do what you need to do" is tacit approval of whatever you want to do—including the one-to-one sessions.

The Communicative Parent Some parents may need to contact you to share what is going on at home. Don't overreact. If they relay good news, be appreciative. If the news is bad, thank them for sharing the information with you. Just be sure that the parents know that the information will be shared with the child. This should not influence your work with the child. It is suggested that you discourage such parent communication because some children may misperceive this as a counselor-parent alliance against them.

> Make certain that, in any explanations or discussion with parents, you do not betray a child's confidences.

The Disruptive Parent Some parents of Children Who Hurt may attempt to sabotage a Trust Building Program. For whatever reasons, they can make unpleasant, critical remarks or innuendos about you to the children. "Hasn't she got anything better to do with her time than see you for a few minutes? Why doesn't she spend time with kids who have *real* problems?" or "You've talked to teachers before. What good will those meetings do anyhow."

Some parents go even further. They protest—go to the school and tell the principal, "I don't want my kids talking alone with that counselor (or teacher)." *If the parent is relentless in trying to stop the one-to-one sessions and the child is caught in the middle, it is best to stop*. Briefly explain your regret or disappointment to the child. There is no need to criticize the parents. Simply explain that parents may prefer that the child do other activities during the time set apart for sessions. "My son needs to be outside," or "My daughter should be with her friends."

If this should happen to you, don't get discouraged. Your experience with this difficult parent helps your understanding of why the child hurts.

Ongoing Positive Feedback

Intermittent Messages Even though a Trust Building Program is child-focused, children want their parents to be proud of them. Intermittent positive feedback to parents can be important. At the same time, as a first step you must inform the child that messages or formal reports are not betrayals of confidences. You will tell the child ahead of time what you will share.

Take time to explain to parents that a child can have

- improved academics with no improvement in behavior.

- no academic progress with improvement in behavior.

- no academic progress, or behavior improvement, but development of the one-to-one relationship with you.

- improved attitude toward work at school with no improvement in attitude toward homework.

Once these contradictions are understood, a parent may be willing to concede that a change of behavior or a finished assignment is improvement.

"It's about time that kid gets his act together. I've been telling him that for a year," the parent may remark.

Your task is not easy. Too large a gap between messages may be perceived by the skeptical parent as "things are not good." The parent might think, "I knew those ongoing private meetings wouldn't amount to anything."

The Sunshine Telephone Call A scheduled, once-a-week *Sunshine Telephone Call* is another feedback strategy. These are two sentence, simple statements about an observed improvement, programmed for a designated time each week. (See Page 200).

It is important that you explain the Sunshine Call plan the first time you call. The parents may be reticent at first to attach any special meaning to the Sunshine Report from you. Once they begin to anticipate calls on a regular basis, the impact of what you share will improve. The plan may be viewed as an indication that you are sincere in wanting them to be informed. A fifth-grade boy reported that things at home improved because of positive messages. His parents no longer called him "problem child" or "stupid."

Rehearse what you may say if a parent is unimpressed by the improvements you report. Use "I" messages. "I enjoy working with your son. Jim works hard on his reports."

Don't personalize it if a parent struggles to accept positive feedback about a child. A defeatist parental attitude is hard to overcome. In some cases, it may take many reports. Every situation is unique.

The Parent-Teacher-Child Conference The Parent-Teacher-Child Conference is another effective way to convey positive messages about school performance (see Page 198).

Because all concerned parties are together, there is no way that the child can manipulate the situation. No one has to accept false blame and all parties can confront excuses for poor performance or inappropriate behavior. All adults know the facts, hear about improvements, explore problems, and ask relevant questions. The adults cannot be manipulated into a competition or a rivalry. There is no opportunity for a home-against-school, or school-against-home drama. A statement such as "She won't help me with my homework" can be addressed the same as the accusation "She never called on me in class. No wonder I got a 'D'."

Adults can hear the child's self-derogatory remarks or pleas for ready praise, sympathy, or attempts to get others to make various excuses on his or her behalf. With the child present, the parent and teacher can decide what encouragement to give the child and how to give it. The adults can decide what strengths to applaud, and the child can ask for what he wants—a positive agenda indeed.

"Please act excited, Mom, if I tell you I got five right on my test. I used to get only three."

"I'd feel better, Ms. Smith, if you would put my art work on the bulletin board. I know it's not as good as some of the other guys, but I like the colors."

There will be some parents who are not interested in attending conferences. Other parents cannot come. Some are basically turned off by anything to do with schools because they have never worked through their own feelings of defeat or anger.

Other Positive Feedback   Smile-O-Grams or Happy Notes that a student is given to take home are crumpled up all too frequently and dropped on the blacktop before the child ever gets on the bus. Younger children, first and second graders, may deliver them to their parents, but by the time a child is in the third grade, Smile-O-Grams have lost their potency. A message that comes through the mail seems to be more noteworthy.

You are capable of judging the progress of a Child Who Hurts. You are a professional who is a keen observer of children.

When You End the Trust Building Program

In the course of your contacts with some parents, you may hear, "It's great to know that someone at school cares about my child." When these parents learn that you are not going to have any more one-to-one sessions with their child, Mom and Dad may be bewildered.

"What happened. Why so soon? We were just getting used to those calls and the encouragement." The parents may feel abandoned. *They may blame the child.* They may accuse their child of being uncooperative or rude as the reason for your ending the one-to-one sessions. Thankfully, at the beginning you did not stipulate a set number of sessions so you are not caught in a numbers game. You may have mentioned the possibility of fourteen to twenty sessions. Be sure to explain to them that your decision is based on improvements that the child displays and tell them about your plan to stay in touch with the child.

Parents need reassurances, too. Tell them you will send occasional positive messages to them. Tell them you would welcome positive feedback from them, too. Thank them for their cooperation. Tell them that their child will always be special to you.

Your willingness to end the one-to-one sessions must be viewed as a vote of confidence to the Child Who Hurts. This is important for parents to know, too.

Communicating With Parents About Parenting

Many Children Who Hurt are living with one or two parents who hurt. Positive feedback about the child may lessen some of that hurt. Parents may also welcome some simple reminders about parenting that can ease tensions in the family. As tensions ease, the parent may better model self-esteem. *Children mirror their parents.* As parents feel better, often the children feel better, too.

The following statements are for information only; not to initiate discussion.

A Parent's Primer

Some Parenting Practices That Work:

- The parent is the family manager. As a manager, he or she will make some decisions that a child likes a lot, and some he or she will not like at all.

- Parenting is not a popularity contest. A parent cannot do everything to please a child.

- Parents have rights, too.

- It is natural that there will be times of misunderstanding and strain between parent and child. Such times may be difficult and leave residual anger, regrets, and/or distancing. Everyone will survive. The relationship will survive—though it may need some changes.

- To repair a relationship after difficulties, be honest with your feelings, explain your needs, find ways to apologize (if necessary) and *determine optimistic pleasant goals together*—backed by plans.

- Children do best when parents act self-assured, follow through, do what they say they will do, are consistent, and model self-discipline and good self-esteem.

You may want to suggest some parenting tapes or books (see Bibliography). Unfortunately, many of the parents of Children Who Hurt are not interested in reading, tapes, meetings, or unsolicited advice or suggestions. They do not attend conferences. This may be discouraging to you. It should serve as reinforcement for your Trust Building Program and your relationship with the child.

8 CHILDREN WHO HATE

All children have moments of frustration in which they "hate" other people. This is not to be confused with the children who have deeprooted, profound problems whom I refer to as *Children Who Hate*.

Many famous names are associated with the understanding of and therapeutic work done with traumatized children. Bruno Bettelheim, Anna Freud, Fritz Redl, David Wineman, and August Aichhorn are among the pioneers who explored the unique needs and problems of children whose controls break down—who defend themselves in antisocial and self-defeating ways.

The deriviation of the hate concept is important. *Hate* goes beyond a response to a "lack of love." *It is a massive reserve of aggression that is not adequately relieved or released through normal channels* such as talking *out* problems, hitting punching bags or other appropriate targets, and so forth. Children Who Hate have unmanageable quantities of aggression, destructiveness, and self-loathing. Some appear empty-eyed and detached from relationships. Many become difficult to love or like. Children Who Hate become the children nobody wants. Many become delinquents. Counselors, teachers, families, and the community at large are unable to put up with what these children do.

Nevertheless, many of these youngsters are in schools and require management. The problems are: 1) how to try to prevent an explosion, 2) how to handle an episode, and 3) how to help a child find acceptable ways to express powerful emotions. (The therapist or staff in a residential setting has two additional tasks—the reconstruction of the child's personality and the restoration of some self-esteem, or the development of sufficient ego-strength to help the child weather provocations, disappointments, and failures.) *Children Who Hate are not candidates for a Trust Building Program. Their needs are too great.*

How to Try to Prevent an Explosion

In a regular classroom it is traditional to specify rules and the consequences that will follow if rules are violated. However, there is no way to conduct a class or handle communication in a group with one hundred percent assurance that an explosive child will not explode. They do not respect authority as others do. Some strategies may work to help the child stay in control, however. Briefly, provide activities with as much built-in instant success and positive reinforcement as possible. Try to monitor the amount of stimuli in the environment—noise, visual distractions, and unstructured activities. Use time-out areas guardedly. Try to keep the volatile child near you so that your reminders or controls may be as quickly or readily forthcoming as possible. Repeat your explanations of workable consequences or discipline whenever necessary. Carry out consequences without apologies. Be cautious about affection and use praise with restraint.

Keep your expectations realistic. Remind yourself that Children Who Hate are not internally directed by right and wrong, fair or unfair, kind or unkind as the others are. When they strike out, they intend to hurt others. Some of their controls have been destroyed by those who hated or betrayed them when they were little, dependent, and weak, and now they are old enough to strike back at anyone.

Take care of yourself. Make certain you have a support person to turn to when you become weary or discouraged.

How to Handle an Explosion

Remove a child from a situation when he or she becomes so aggressive that no technique results in control. Do not display anger. Force may be necessary to get the child under control. Do *not* use *hurtful* force. Stay with the child to help him or her cope with feelings about removal.

Do not create a "new scene" by having more than two adults converge on the child at one time. You must react to and manage the situation. An outburst will seldom stop on its own or wear itself out. When these children lose control, it will accelerate. The upset child does not pay attention to words or threats. You have to be involved physically.

How to Help a Child Find an Acceptable Way to Express Powerful Feelings in the Classroom

Many kids who are upset may be able to keep from hitting and being destructive if they scream, swear, or make wild threats. Unpleasant and difficult as this may be, it is a marked improvement from their hurting others or themselves. Do not overreact to the content. See the outburst as a "letting off of steam." You may even want to say, "Calling somebody a _____ is lots better than slamming someone around."

You are not a therapist. At some point you may want to take time to talk about the content of the screams, but intense, introspective interviews are not expected.

Other appropriate outlets that work for some kids include the use of punching bags, trampolines, running, calisthenics, or throwing snowballs at a tree or digging in the dirt. Do not placate with special favors or ingratiate. Such acceptance can be *too contrasting*, when compared to the deprivation, neglect, or cruelty this child may have known in the past or is still experiencing at home. Be cool. Be professional. Be managerial. In special classes where groups are small and contacts intense, the involvement and affect of the adult may become ingratiating and endearing more readily. There may be many opportunities for uninterrupted conversations and sensitive sharing.

Children Who Hate—In Therapy

Some Children Who Hate are not workable. They may become hardened criminals, psychopaths, sociopaths, or a statistic in a morgue file. Others can be helped. There is no one definitive therapeutic method to help these children recover. Some methods work only in a regulated, residential setting. Others require a punitive environment such as a detention center. Some are effective in a psychiatric hospital. A few will respond to outpatient help in combination with medications and supervision. Whatever the method, the goals are the same: reestablishment of controls, repair or strengthening of a sense of self-worth, of the ego, in conjunction with the capacity to relate to others with a degree of comfort.

Children Who Hate are the victims of dysfunctional parenting and/or life's circumstances. One must search hard for their wellness—in some cases, this is an indescribably difficult task. To get them to acknowledge their strengths and wellness may be impossible. We have an obligation to do what we can do along the way. With compassion; *remember—someone threw rocks at their rainbows.*

EPILOGUE: A NOTE OF THANKS

There are so many children who need to learn to trust one adult in order to feel good about themselves. There are so many adults who want to be that special person to Children Who Hurt. Thank you for being one of these. I know that you are because you selected this book to read; this program to follow. I am certain that your successes in Trust Building programs will enhance your good feelings about yourself.

At the same time, there is a sadness and regret; sadness because there are so many child victims from homes rife with conflicts and sorrow, and regret that we cannot reach all of them. We can only do what we can do.

But, if five teachers in every school had six or eight Trust Building Programs per year, imagine the number of kids who could be helped. What an exciting prospect! That's why I wrote this book.

Thanks to all of you for your efforts on behalf of the Shellys, Rogers, Tims and Marys that *you* know.

Thank you for being so caring.

SELF-CONCEPT ACTIVITIES FOR ADULTS AND CHILDREN

Take Care of You

Affirmations Are Important

My Self-esteem at its Best—Questions with answers which denote healthy self-esteem

Compliment Training—A program for adults and children

"Me" A Self-concept Learning Station—(Student Activities)

All About Me—Language Arts Experience—Sample contract with self

The Choice of Praise or Encouragement—The rationale for the use of encouragement

Respect in the Classroom

TAKE CARE OF YOU

Your commitment to a Trust Building Program is built around hope. Your commitment implies that you will keep going regardless of obstacles, discouragement, or frustrations. Ask yourself, "What have I got to lose if I give up on this student?" Then ask, "What does he or she have to lose if I don't even try?" The answers will undoubtedly inspire you to persevere.

Your frustrations or disappointment are all too real. They can interfere with your enthusiasm unless you have ongoing support for yourself. Who are *your* support persons? What do you share? What do you need or want? Do you follow their suggestions such as to relax, take breaks, diversify, take time to play, enjoy the work you do, the kids you know, meditate—celebrate your success? Such suggestions offered by support persons enrich your emotional well-being.

Your positive answers to the following questions may provide energy—perhaps excitement. They are intended to be supportive and encouraging.

My friends choose me as a friend because I (tell great jokes, am loyal, etc.) _____

_____

_____

By participating in a one-to-one Trust Building Program, I feel (creative, appreciated, hopeful, worthy, etc.) _____

_____

_____

Four things I like about myself physically are (the color of my hair, etc.) _____

_____

_____

My greatest talents as a counselor (teacher, speech therapist, social worker, etc.) are

_____

_____

_____

I nurture my intellectual interests in the following ways: _____

_____

_____

_____

I am aware of a mind-body-spirit interrelatedness. I care for my body by _____

_____

_____

Three things I did for myself:
Last year _____

_____

_____

Last month _____

_____

_____

Yesterday _____

_____

_____

Three goals I would like to achieve:

Goal (such as)	Approximate time
(Trip to Vancouver) _____	(next summer) _____
(Finish reupholstering chair) _____	eight weeks _____
(Start progressive letter to sister, grandparent) _____	(next weekend) _____

I understand that the word assertive means that I can act or ask for what I want in an appropriate way. I can stick up for myself. I need to be more assertive in these types

of situations:_____

_____

_____

I am comfortable with the fact that everyone needs guidance or instruction occasion

ally. When I feel frustrated or want advice, I turn to _____

_____

_____

AFFIRMATIONS ARE IMPORTANT; USE AFFIRMATIONS FOR YOURSELF

Special support for yourself includes the use of affirmations and the self-esteem questions. Affirmations are positive statements that you repeat to yourself to applaud who you are and what good things you do. They may be written down or recited out loud. You may employ more than one affirmation at a time. Some are sensitive and some superficial. Enjoy! But use them!

Sample Affirmations:

"I deserve to talk about myself as a way of enriching a child's understanding of adults."

"I deserve to buy some out-of-season fresh strawberries after school." "I managed to stay focused on Randy when he was telling about his dad hitting his mom. I wanted to say something judgmental but I didn't."

"I deserve to acknowledge that I'm learning a lot about Children Who Hurt every time I meet with Randy."

"I deserve to have someone listen to my comments and experiences with Randy and Nancy. These experiences are very important to me."

Be generous with your affirmations to yourself. You may want to record them in a journal.

Affirmations confirm who you are. They are a tool to help change old, negative attitudes. They support improvements and help build self-esteem.

An action plan for taking care of yourself can be readily structured based on your answers to all the questions in this section. Identify your "weak" spots and arrange to strengthen them—one at a time.

> **At the beginning of this book, the question was asked, "If you don't help the Child Who Hurts, who will?" An appropriate question now is—"If I don't take care of me, who will?"**

Learning to trust is a process—an experience. It cannot be learned from a description on a page or words from a speech.

Thanks to you, your students will learn about the Trust Building Process. No small feat!

MY SELF-ESTEEM AT ITS BEST

- *Do I ask for what I want?* "I'm making spaghetti tonight because I *want* spaghetti." "I want you to be quiet. I've been involved with people all day."

- *Do I do things for me?* "I'm going to soak in the bathtub for a few minutes before I help you with your homework." "I'm going to call Jane on the phone. She's my best friend. I always feel better after I talk to her."

- *Do I save some money and use it for myself?* "I've been wanting a new pair of black pantyhose. I'm going to buy them from the grocery money. I earn the money. I'm entitled to spend some on myself."

- *Do I take time to be creative?* "It's been months since I wrote a poem or a long letter. I like to write. I'm going to do that tonight instead of watching TV."

- *Do I express what I like or do not like without feeling guilty?* "I hate violence on TV. I will change the channel when a violent show comes on. I will also be 'stronger' with the kids and take charge of what they watch.

- *I am okay if I can't answer a child's question about something I don't know.* "I'll never understand how a microwave works. I may ask someone, look it up, go to the library, or have the kids ask somebody else. There is *too much* to know today. I am okay if I can't talk about marine biology or explain how computers work."

- *I am learning to forgive myself.* "So I made a mistake or a poor decision—that's how life is. I'm *human*. Sometimes I feel bad; really guilty, and have remorse, but I've learned that everyone makes mistakes."

- *I do the best that I can do. There is no one "right" way to be a parent.* There are many ways to manage a family and I can only be me. I don't want to be compared with anyone else nor do I want some writer in a book to tell me everything I'm supposed to do or not do. I like suggestions, but I have to be me."

- *If I can't sort things out, I'll ask for help.* "I don't feel like a failure if I ask for help when I need it."

- *I read that parents are supposed to be consistent. Here's what I think.* "My dad was calm, quiet, and distant. My mother was outgoing and energetic. Dad was strict, Mom was not. I'm inconsistent, but *consistently* inconsistent."

Manifestations of good self-esteem are manifestations of wellness. Be proud!

COMPLIMENT TRAINING

All people need to learn to give and take compliments.

1. Explain the program to the class, stressing that giving and accepting compliments will feel funny at first but will become increasingly comfortable. State that the purpose of the exercise is to help everyone become more comfortable in the give and take of sincere commendation and acknowledgment.

   Be firm when you remind the group that there will be no put-downs, sarcastic remarks, or grimaces. This rule should already be established in the classroom.

2. Have adults model compliments to each other for initial demonstration for the entire class. One adult gives a compliment to another, for all to hear.

   Rationale: If you demonstrate with one student only, another student may feel injured, slighted, or unworthy.

3. Model compliments on three levels: *superficial, interpersonal, and personal.*

Examples:

- "I like that shirt you are wearing." (superficial)

- "The way you help Frances with her math is great." (interpersonal)

- "You have a lot of patience." (personal)

Code the three levels so the students will understand

Example:

- Superficial will be called "A"

- Interpersonal "B"

- Personal "C"

4. Tell the students to exchange a compliment with a seatmate or partner when the Compliment Clock goes off. The Compliment Clock is a kitchen timer that you set to go off at intermittent times, though not every day. Times should be determined by the seating

arrangement of the students so that different students will interact with each other (not the same pairs repeatedly).

5. Encourage private record-keeping so that students may note the nice things that many of their peers and others, too, say about them.

6. Utilize the compliments for work in language arts, art, humor, cartoons, drama, miniskits, and the like.

7. Participate yourself. This adds an important dimension to your relationship with the students.

One teacher from Oregon has originated a system that she has used for "Classroom Compliments." She seats five students at five large tables. Her plan: If each table secures 6 compliments per day, each table member is entitled to 15 minutes free time at the close of the day.

Compliments can be given for:

* helping others

* written work

* positive behavior

* encouraging, supportive interactions

* tidiness

Compliments can be given by:

* classroom teacher

* other teachers, e.g., P.E., music, art

* parents, volunteers, aides

This program helps peers do well to earn the score needed.

After an individual has learned to acknowledge compliments from others without embarrassment or denial, he or she may be more open to getting in touch with his own talents and positive attributes. It will also benefit the student to utilize praise from those teachers with whom he or she may be uncomfortable or whom he does not like at all.

Compliment training is quick and sometimes superficial, but it is effective. Compliments from peers enrich or validate the commendations the Child Who Hurts hears in one-to-one sessions.

Idea!
"Me"
A Self-Concept Learning Station

Objective: Through reading, writing, and oral expression, the student will direct himself toward building a positive self-concept.

Activities:

1. Write a poem or paragraph to describe something about yourself that no one at school knows about.

2. Write a poem about some of your feelings—what makes you happy, sad, angry, etc.

3. Draw a picture to show what you do when you have no one else to play with.

4. Make a list of six things that make you wonder the most and then share this list with a friend.

5. Write a joke or draw a picture about something you think is funny. Share this with a friend.

6. Draw a picture of yourself. How do you see yourself?

7. Relate, to a friend or group, a positive experience about yourself.

8. Write a paragraph using good adjectives to describe your best friend or someone in your group.

9. Read a book or short story about someone who has overcome great difficulty.

Sample Contract
Language-Arts Experience—All About Me

Objectives: 1. To get to know, understand, and love myself better.
2. To get to know, understand, and love other people better.

Options:

1. Have a friend draw a silhouette (shadow outline) of me using an overhead projector or bright lamp. Then do the same for my friend.

2. Write a few sentences on my silhouette about the things I think about.

3. Write the things I like to see, hear, or taste on my silhouette.

4. Write what things I'm most interested in on my silhouette.

5. From the TV guide in the daily newspaper, choose the show I would most like to see. Write a paragraph why I like it.

(or)

Write a review of my favorite TV show to convince other kids to watch it.

(or)

Write a TV commercial for my favorite show. Get a group of kids to act it out.

6. Write a poem about something I really care about.

7. If I had a million dollars, how would I spend it? Write a paragraph about it or discuss it with a group.

8. Write a book review about my favorite book, encourage other students to read it.

9. Prepare a talk and/or a small display about my hobby for other kids who might be interested in learning about it and how to get started.

10. Draw a picture and/or write a poem about something I like to see, hear, smell, taste, or touch.

11. Bring in a series of pictures of me and talk about my early adventures.

12. Write a short play or skit in which the characters are "me," "myself," and "I."

13. If I could live anywhere in the U.S.A., what place would I choose and why? Write a composition about it or have a discussion. Include things about the history and environment of the place.

14. Sketch a map of the U.S.A. Show on it, with a symbol of my own choice, all the places that my family's relatives (aunts, uncles, etc.) live.

15. On the center of a large map of the U.S.A., put a pin flag with my last name on it, in the place my father or mother was born.

16. What is my favorite sport? Explain why on the silhouette of a player or a piece of that sport's equipment (and/or) make a collage of words that belong to my favorite sport. Cut pictures, words, etc. from magazines, newspaper headlines, or draw some of my own. See how many people know the meaning of these words.

17. Other_____

_____

_____

       Date started_____

       Student_____

       Teacher_____

I plan to complete this contract by_____

       Date completed_____

       Student_____

       Teacher_____

THE CHOICE OF PRAISE OR
ENCOURAGEMENT*

PRAISE:	*ENCOURAGEMENT:*
1. Is general. "You are a great kid."	1. Is specific. "You got eight out of ten right."
2. Is judgmental. "That's a great job."	2. Is descriptive. The goal is to allow the student to do the judging. "I noticed that you were taking turns on the playground today."
3. Places value upon the quality of of the performance or the product. "I really like that paper."	3. Emphasizes and values effort. "I bet you worked hard on this one."
4. Emphasizes the feelings of the person doing the praising. "I'm so proud of the way you work in school."	4. Emphasizes the feelings of the student. "Wow, five out of five! I bet that feels great!"
5. Is often manipulative. However, this depends upon the intentions of the person doing the praising and the perceptions of the person being praised.	5. Avoids manipulation since the student does most of the judging.
6. Works only when the student believes that the praise is accurate and sincere. Praise creates cognitive dissonance in students who have a low self-concept.	6. Is the technique of choice for students who have a low self-concept. This technique reduces the chance of cognitive dissonance.

* Jim Fay. *Success With the Reluctant Learner*, 2207 Jackson St., Golden, CO 80401: School Consultant Services, Inc.

RESPECT IN THE CLASSROOM

To enhance a child's self-esteem, the teacher must make certain that every child feels respected. Throughout the school year or semester together, the students must be reminded of the following important statements:

- There will be no *put-downs* in this class.

- There will be *no teasing* in this class.

- No one is to be belittled for asking for help. At some time, in some way, everyone needs help.

- Prejudicial slurs, or name-calling will not be tolerated.

- If a person cries or seems upset, that person is not to be criticized. Some people are more emotional than others.

- Do not criticize shy people. Shyness often means that a student is afraid. A shy person cannot be persuaded to be "unshy." It takes time and trust.

- Everyone makes mistakes. Do not laugh at someone who makes a mistake. If you make a mistake, you may feel discouraged. Learn to say, "Everyone makes mistakes" and try again, using more effort if necessary.

- Nobody in this class is any more important than any other person.

- Even though I am an adult, I have feelings, too.

- If someone has made an error in the past, that is history. Reminders of past problems are disrespectful.

When students feel respected and protected, you, the teacher, have achieved a positive classroom climate. This may inspire children to put forth more effort to learn, and may make them more receptive to what you can provide.

APPENDIX: PART 2
DETAILED PROCEDURES FOR ACTIVITIES TO ENHANCE
A TRUST BUILDING PROGRAM

Limits for the Total Class: Negotiated Rules for Everybody

Students Teaching Students: A program enabling the student to tutor a younger child. Feedback from a younger child is important reinforcement to a Child Who Hurts.

Contract Learning: How to Proceed

Pretesting and Post testing: How to Proceed

The Parent-Teacher-Child Conference: How to Proceed

The Sunshine Telephone Call: (Teacher to Parent)

Limits for the Total Class

Stable Limits—Negotiated Rules for Everybody *This school is nothing but a bunch of rules and regulations. Every day it's something new!* This is not true when a classroom is managed by *stable limits*.

The Child Who Hurts derives a special message from the classroom managed by stable limits: that rules and consequences are for everyone. Stable limits help a teacher to be consistent. This adds to his or her credibility. It helps the Child Who Hurts learn to trust.

Establishing stable limits is not difficult. **Purpose:**

- To provide limits for everyone in the class.

- To clarify that rules are for all students.

- To set the tone of the class.

- To prevent arbitrary discipline.

- To build mutual respect.

Negotiating Stable Limits The teacher writes his/her items on the board in one column. The students write their items in an adjacent column. Together they will select an equal number from each list, the number dependent on the age of students and the existing problems in the classroom. No more than five limits should be considered at one time. *Consequences for violations should also be negotiated.*

Your List (5)	**Student's List (5)**
Come in on time	Field trips—2 per month
Be courteous	Chew gum
No name-calling or put-downs	No homework on weekends
Put names on papers or no grades will be given	Interest centers—Thursday afternoons
No hitting	Choose own seatmates

Public Notice All stable limits are to be kept posted at all times. Each student is asked to make a copy for him- or herself and keep one for parents.

Renegotiations These may be initiated by the students or the teacher at any time.

Ongoing Use of Stable Limits Read the rules or limits frequently so that there will be no misunderstanding of either content or intent.

The stable limits, or limits for the total class, provide an additional service to a Child Who Hurts—*peer pressure.* One half of the rules and consequences are determined by the kids, *not* the adults. The Child Who Hurts may trust peers and the limits they set. Some consequences will be rewards or special favors. The child may also accept peer pressure to follow the stable limits so that the whole class will be rewarded.

Operating within the framework of stable limits provides distance between the child and adult which may be beneficial. If a student perceives the Trust Building Program to be stultifying, the limits for the total class may be perceived as breathing space. There is no way to predict how a student may vacillate in his or her perceptions of closeness, distance, smothering, or structure. It is predictable that these perceptions will vary and will affect your working relationship at some point.

Students Teaching Students

The Child Who Hurts May Tutor a Younger Person

Procedures

The Steps:	Reasons:
1. Ask the student whom he/she would like to tutor. Possible scenario: "I'd like to help a third-grade girl with her math."	1. The more input the student has, the greater the chance to create interest, even enthusiasm, the more he/she senses respect from the teachers. The answers, in a sense, "load the deck" toward success.
2. Teacher (Counselor) contacts teacher of the younger child. Possible scenario: Mr. Atkins contacts third-grade teacher—makes arrangements for Tim to "interview" her and makes plans for working with Susie. When Mr. Atkins reports that he takes the first steps, he adds, "It's an important task to help someone, Tim. I'm sure you'll do a good job. I'm here to offer suggestions if you need them."	2. Student is involved in the planning—not told what to do. Supervision will be nominal once the pattern of the tutoring sessions has been established.
3. Child Who Hurts interviews teacher of younger child to find out what is being taught and what materials are needed. Tutor's special problems may be discussed. Possible scenario: Materials needed may require student to find film strip, make puzzles, or math games. "Tim, Susie learns with her hands and she acts very upset every time she makes a mistake. If she writes her answers on a small, lap-size chalkboard and can erase	3. The Child Who Hurts assumes responsibility or ownership for his/her role as a tutor. The needs of the younger child may require the student to brush up on his/her own skills, learn new ones, or learn how to make explanations, be patient, accept mistakes, etc. The setup for the interview is based on the confidence and respect of the faculty involved. Making materials is an important learning process—whether for math,

them immediately, she will not focus on a wrong answer." Tim is excited about meeting Susie and borrows some worksheets and answer sheets from the teacher so that he can practice the lessons.

4. Develop a plan: Provide a kitchen timer—review instructions with student. Break up the tutoring time into workable units. Possible scenario: Tim will work with Susie from 10–10:35 twice a week for 4 weeks. 10–10:10 Math; 10:10 kitchen timer goes off. 10:10—10:20 Alternative Planned Activity—e.g., puzzles, talk ("My parents got divorced. I know yours did, too. How are you doing?"). Read comics together, play quick games, or start others. 10:20 Kitchen timer goes off. 10:20–10:30 Math (This adds up to 20 minutes tutoring time—satiation for both students.) 10:30 Kitchen timer goes off. 10:30—10:35 Review, finish Alternative Activity, prepare homework lesson, etc. 10:35 Depart.

social studies, spelling, or whatever. When the student uses the materials and understands how these benefit the needy younger child, they produce positive reinforcement, "I'm a helper."

4. Without a plan, the Child Who Hurts may feel insecure. This can be prevented by following Step 4. It is unfair to ask a student to develop his/her own plan, especially if he/she has a short attention span, tends to be disorganized, or can't visualize how long it takes to make explanations, show examples, give directions, etc. A plan diminishes anxiety. A plan gives the student important structure and enhances a sense of competency. Small units defer to the shorter attention span of the younger child and possible problems of the Child Who Hurts. Talk will be quiet—confidential. You may be the only person the younger student can confide in—*or smile with*. Planned activity means no one will be disturbing the rest of the class; no walking around, acting silly, or making noises. (*continued*)

5. Keep records. The Child Who Hurts will keep the records as affirmation of what tasks have been handled and what learning has taken place. Possible scenario: Diary Record: Day one—Susie asked me why I came. I said, "To teach you math," She said, "Okay." Day two—Susie said, "I'm glad to see you."

5. Children Who Hurt may respond to encouragement and disbelieve praise. A written record of achievements provides data and encouragement. Careful notes denote effort and goals that are met. The records may have far greater impact on the student's low self-esteem than praise. Students who do not trust are wary of praise—see it as manipulative or phony. Subjective dialogue (with positive feelings) is an important affirmation that the Child Who Hurts has done a good job. Feedback from peers is especially necessary until the student has learned to trust adults.

Contract Learning
Procedure

Ask the student, "What do you want to learn?" Outline the curricula mandates or skills needed, incorporating the child's desires as the basis for the parameters of the contract. Approximately 60% of the "What" decision will be predetermined, but the student will have the right to negotiate and decide the other 40%. He or she may need your help with this. It may be a new (and exciting) experience.

Example: 5th Grade Social Studies Unit

Topic: The Fishing Industry

Student ideas or suggestions:

Special problems with salmon	Effects of pollution
Disaster at sea	Fishing laws
Life of Jack London	Old equipment, new equipment
Life in a fishing village	Maintenance of canneries
Fishing as a job	

If the Child Who Hurts had received the assignment, "I want you to write a report on the Fishing Industry and have it ready in three weeks," the chances are he or she might have done nothing. Or the child might conscientiously copy three paragraphs or sentences out of a book. By encouraging the child to select a small aspect of the topic, assuring him or her that he or she will receive full credit for work, he or she will feel secure enough to put forth more than cursory effort. Together you take the content or task and break it up into "academic options" for the student to select and pursue. If the student is resistant or disinterested or declares he or she doesn't want to do anything, it may be essential for you to declare that you have the responsibility to find a way to help him or her make choices. It is appropriate to comment, "It's part of my job to make this subject, or a part of it, interesting to you, and then come up with suggestions for how to get you to do your end of the work." This approach is more respectful than asking a student to choose one of the topics listed at the end of a chapter and proceed with a report.

What materials will you need to complete the contract?

This question is intended to help the teacher and student find or supply appropriate materials. The choice permits a child who does not like to read other modalities for completing work. Usually, the materials selected reflect the child's preferred learning style, whether auditory, kinesthetic, or visual. He or she may have to be responsible for finding many of the materials alone (depending on age) or making them. Again, the child is presented options for how he or she is to perform academic tasks. Many anxious Children Who Hurt overreact to paper-pencil tasks. They need a chance to use a tape recorder, write on a blackboard, or make hands-on exhibits. A series of drawings or one line topic sentences that a child puts on clear film for filmstrip use can prove to be highly motivating, especially if the child may look forward to showing this to a group or perhaps to the whole class.

Who do you want to work with?

Be cautious. If you are aware that the student may be brutally rejected if he invites others to work with him, then do not offer the option. It would further hurt a child who already hurts. On the other hand, an opportunity to work with a best friend or neighbor may be inspirational, resulting in enthusiasm to get started and in completion.

"This is the first time. I've ever worked with Louie," a student may exclaim. "He's in the fast reading group." When two or more students work together they develop a *group contract*, and while they work together, you are free to assist other students.

How long do you think you will need to finish the contract?

The reason for contract learning is to program a Child Who Hurts into *success experiences*. The time options must be realistic in order for a child to experience success.

The teacher assumes the role of being a sensitive guide. If the youngster wants three days to do five short math problems, that may be too much time. Negotiations ending in agreement for too much time will inadvertently give the Child Who Hurts the impression that he cannot do well or is, perhaps, an unusually slow learner. The student will not concentrate on the fact that the work may be difficult or complicated. He will see the long-time agreement as an insult. Too little time, on the other hand, may prove discouraging. Renegotiate when necessary. The first contracts must be short. Subsequent time limits can be lengthened or adjusted to the improved interest or attention span.

How shall we evaluate your work?

The contract offers a Child Who Hurts a chance to negotiate his or her own success. The completed contract is not phony. It represents commitment and fulfillment, and the grade must convey these achievements. It may be the first assignment the student has attempted or completed in months. It is not intended to pit one student against another.

In introducing the students to contract learning, stress that it is intended to be basically noncompetitive. "You, Jim, have a contract to draw a set of pictures depicting the old fishing tackle used by the Eskimo while Henry will write a brief history of the fishing methods used by the Japanese. Your grade will not be based on one contract entirely unless we decide that together. A number of contracts will give us a better idea of what you have learned and what a good job you have done." For a different example: "Mark, I want you to learn to like math. I'm certain you will feel pleased when you have two or three papers all done and ninety percent correct. How would you feel about starting with only five problems and we'll call that an 'A'? I t doesn't matter that Kenny is doing twelve problems. He likes math. It's his favorite subject and that's the contract that we agreed on."

Kids will talk and compare contracts. Do not become discouraged. You have the right to help each student according to his needs. Contracts may be a beginning step in motivating an unmotivated boy or girl.

In summary:

- Contracts can be either written or oral.

- Contracts may be written by the student(s) or teacher or presented in standardized, printed form, pages of a book, questions at the bottom of a page or test items from a pretest the student has taken.

- Contracts can be either individual or group.

- Contracts, or parts thereof, can be renegotiated at any time.

- Contracts can be used for enrichment or extra credit.

Remember, if a student fails to complete a contract, *it is the wrong contract*. Some part of it did not meet his or her needs at the time it was negotiated, or he or she did not master the skills he needed to proceed.

Renegotiation does not represent failure. it is further evidence of your commitment to the student's success.

No, it is not necessary that the student have a contract for every day However, at the onset of a Trust Building Program, it is essential that the student have learning tasks that he or she can master of which he or she can feel proud. A contract constructed with the student has impact: As a joint venture, the child's input, combined with your own, will be essential keys to success for your program.

Pretesting and Post-Testing

This is a teaching technique to help a Child Who Hurts experience academic success. The test contains skills that most students have mastered and some familiar content. It decreases anxiety as it introduces new information, tasks, or skills which are to be mastered. Thus, it becomes a presentation of facts; the specifics of what is ahead. When the child knows what is ahead, he is less fearful than when presented with unanticipated lessons or assignments.

Before the test is distributed, announce to the class, "This is an activity or a test to determine what you know and what you do not know. You will not be graded. We will develop individual contracts or group units or lesson plans for you based on what you need. At the end of this unit, you will be tested again. I am trying to take the worry out of school."

Return the corrected pretests to the student as promised. Proceed to develop a plan. Have the student make a list: "This is what I need to learn." Select one or two items (skills) at a time and plan accordingly. The plan may be incorporated into a contract, or you may simply spell out the materials to be used, time, and so forth. When the student is involved in the planning stage, it nullifies the assumption that this is just *another* teacher assignment. Involvement is a learning process that can lead to both commitment and excitement.

Check out the child's skills before he or she starts, and allow time for explanation as part of the plan. If the student confronts a problem that he or she immediately recognizes as being too hard, feelings of inadequacy will be reinforced. You will hear, "I can't do it—won't even try. I'm afraid." Give necessary instruction, then specify periodic check-in times to make certain the student is proceeding accurately. When independent study time is divided into time units (for example, every five minutes), the student gets the message that his or her success *is* important to you. Such close check-ins may be necessary for three to four school weeks. After that, the student can probably concentrate for longer stretches.

The retest is an indicator of learning and achievement. Consider giving the *pretest, post-test, or final test* in a different modality than the original paper-pencil test.

Alternative methods:

- Let the student dictate answers into a tape recorder.

- Let the student write answers on the board.

- Let the student teach what has been mastered to another student.

- Let the student tell you what has been learned.

- Let the student make new materials to demonstrate what has been learned.

If it is necessary or planned to use the original test, do just that. The student will feel successful as he or she handles the questions or problems which were either left blank or incorrect the first time around.

Educators hope that students will become successful test takers but that is but one of their goals. All methods are intended to improve the damaged self-esteem of Children Who Hurt. The use of tests must be considered among the skills that teachers teach.

Using test items as teaching materials is another technique to help a Child Who Hurts experience success in academics. It does not invalidate what is learned. The teacher presents sample test items or problems to the child for explanation, drill, or mastery as part of the ongoing classroom curriculum. When the child is presented with the test, the questions feel familiar and anxiety is diminished, if not eliminated. The purpose of tests is to measure what the children have learned; not to scare them so that they cannot perform well.

THE PARENT-TEACHER-CHILD CONFERENCE

Recommended Procedures:

1. Involve the student in all the planning. Have the student issue the invitation, collect contracts, art work, etc.

2. Share with the student, ahead of time, all the material and comments you will tell his or her parents—comments both positive and negative, or critical.

Again, the element of surprise must be carefully considered. If you make a nice remark about Harry and Harry is not prepared, his first thought may be, "She only said that for my mom's benefit. It really isn't true," or, "How come she didn't tell me that she was going to tell my mom about that?"

It is as if there are barriers to his acknowledging positive feedback from his teacher into his own feedback receptors.

3. Let the student conduct the conference.

Preplan guidelines: The conference is not a time to rehash the past.

The purpose of the conference is to share assessment with parents—to make certain that home and school are equally well informed of a student's progress.

A further purpose is to establish new goals or objectives. Inform the student that his or her parents may wish to be involved in certain contracts. The ultimate decision about parental involvement should be negotiated by all three parties.

4. At the onset of the conference it may be wise to read over, with the parents, the stable limits from which the management of your class proceeds.

The parents will have already received a copy. It is worth rereading the section on no put-downs as a way of preventing sarcastic or rude remarks that a parent may be tempted to make about the child during the conference.

A conference is not a forum in which each person takes turns ventilating feelings. It is for planning and should serve as additional support to the student, the student-family communication and the Trust Building Program.

5. If a parent wants to bring up issues not directly related to the student and school progress, make arrangements for a private meeting at another time.

6. If you have arranged for the Child Who Hurts to be free of grades and a parent asks for grade equivalents or level of reading or math, don't hesitate to express your reasons for nongrading decisions. If the child has a learning problem or dysfunction and is doing below-grade-level work, both he and his parents are aware of this. It has been demonstrated that students with learning disabilities frequently do catch up in high school or at least acquire adequate skills for vocational survival. *Try* to be reassuring to parents. Focus on growth, effort, and achievements in order to assist them in not overreacting to deficiencies and problems. Point out that test scores may be a misrepresentation because of the child's anxiety about tests.

THE SUNSHINE TELEPHONE CALL

1. Tell the student ahead of time exactly when you will be calling and what you will be sharing with his or her parents.

2. In the first call to the parents clarify that: The *purpose* is to report something positive about the student. Identify it as a Sunshine Call. "I'm calling to tell you that Louis was most helpful when visitors came today." The *plan*: A one or two sentence report on a predetermined basis, "I'll be calling you on the first and third Friday of every month to report something Louis has achieved or done well." The *content*: Either academic or nonacademic, "Some calls may be about Louis' work and some about other things. I do not discuss problems in a Sunshine Call."

3. Guard against going beyond the one or two sentence limit. Otherwise calls may get long or off-topic, and you will be discouraged from calling again.

4. Prepare yourself for a myriad of parental responses. Some mothers may cry. You may hear, "This is the first nice call I have had from the school." If parents are sarcastic or belittling, ignore it. Their uncertainty is to be expected.

5. Make brief notes of "content of call" for written feedback in case it may be meaningful at some time in the future. Such notations may be necessary to use should misunderstandings arise or for amplification in a parent-teacher-child conference.

6. Parents of older students may be less interested in calls than parents of younger children. *Your consistency and acceptance of parental response will stabilize the school-home feedback system.*

7. *Note:* If the parents seem displeased or dissatisfied or demand further time or clarification, arrange for a conference. A parent may answer, "It's about time Louis is polite in school. But how is he doing in math?" Teacher's answer: "The Sunshine Call is to report good news. We are working on Louis' math. We'll look at his math progress at a conference."

IN SOME WAYS, HOWEVER SMALL AND SECRET

IN SOME WAYS, HOWEVER SMALL AND SECRET
EACH OF US IS A LITTLE MAD.
EVERYONE IS LONELY AT BOTTOM, AND CRIES TO BE UNDERSTOOD.
BUT WE CAN NEVER ENTIRELY UNDERSTAND SOMEONE ELSE
AND EACH OF US REMAINS PART STRANGER, EVEN TO THOSE WHO
  LOVE US.

IT IS THE WEAK WHO ARE CRUEL.
GENTLENESS CAN ONLY BE EXPECTED FROM THE STRONG.
THOSE WHO DO NOT KNOW FEAR, ARE NOT REALLY BRAVE,
FOR COURAGE IS THE CAPACITY TO CONFRONT WHAT CAN BE
  IMAGINED.
AND YOU CAN UNDERSTAND PEOPLE BETTER IF YOU LOOK AT THEM,
NO MATTER HOW OLD, OR IMPRESSIVE THEY ARE
AS IF THEY ARE CHILDREN.
FOR MOST OF US NEVER REALLY MATURE, WE SIMPLY GROW TALLER.
AND HAPPINESS COMES ONLY WHEN WE PUSH OUR HEARTS AND
  BRAINS
TO THE FARTHEST REACHES OF WHICH WE ARE CAPABLE.
FOR THE PURPOSE OF LIFE IS TO MATTER, TO COUNT,
TO STAND FOR SOMETHING,
TO HAVE IT MAKE SOME DIFFERENCE THAT YOU LIVE
AT ALL.

LEO RALSTON

REFERENCES

Arent, Ruth P. and Michelle Kory Waters. *Kids: You Can Manage Your Own Stress!*, P.O. Box 2SOl, Littleton, CO 80161: 1982.

Arent, Ruth P. *Stress and Your Child*, Englewood Cliffs, NJ: Prentice Hall, 1984.

Arent, Ruth P. *Take Time To Talk*, Denver, CO: The Lynn Press, 1989.

Armstrong, Louise. *How to Turn War into Peace: A Child's Guide to Conflict Resolution*, New York: Harcourt Brace Jovanovich, 1979.

The *Assist* Program. *Building Self-Concept in The Classroom*, Seattle: Pat Huggins, 1986.

Carlson, Jon and Casey Thorpe. *The Growing Teacher*, Englewood Cliffs, NJ: Prentice Hall, 1984.

Carter Jay. *Nasty People*, New York: Contemporary Books, 1979.

Cedoline, Anthony, J. *The Effect of Affect*, San Rafael, CA: Academic Therapy Publications, 1977.

Cohen, Alan. *Have You Hugged a Monster Today?*, P.O. Box 5658, Somerset, N.J. 08875: Alen Cohen Publications, 1982.

Eberle, Bob and Rose Emery Hall. *Affective Education Guidebook*, East Aurora, N.Y.: D.0.K. Publishers, 197S.

Fagen, Stanley A., Nicholas J. Long, and Donald J. Stevens. *Teaching Children Self-Control*, Columbus, Ohio: Charles E. Merrill, 1975.

Fay, Jim. *Success With The Reluctant Learner*, 2207 Jackson St., Golden, CO 8O40l: School Consultant Services, Inc., 1985.

Fay, Jim. *Tickets to Success*, 2207 Jackson St., Golden, CO 80401: Cline/Fay Institute, 1988.

Firth, Terry. *Secrets Parents Should Know About Public Schools*, New York: Simon and Schuster, 1985.

Garmezy, Norman, et al. *Stress, Coping and Development in Children*, New York: McGraw-Hill 1983.

Gartner, Alan, Mary Kohler, and Frank Riessman. *Children Teach Children,* New York: Harper and Row, 1971

Hayes, E. Kent. *Why Good Parents Have Bad Kids,* New York: Doubleday, 1989.

Jampolsky, Gerald. *Love is Letting Go of Fear,* New York: Bantam Books, 1979.

Krumboltz, John D. and Helen B. Krumboltz. *Changing Children's Behavior,* Englewood Cliffs, NJ: Prentice Hall, 1972.

Magdid, Ken and Carole A. McKelvey. *High Risk Children Without a Conscience,* New York: Bantam Books, 1987.

Moorman, Chick and Dee Dishon. *Our Classroom: We Can Learn Together,* Englewood Cliffs, NJ: Prentice Hall, 1983.

Palenski, Joseph E. *Kids Who Run Away,* P.O. Box 2008, Saratoga, CA: R & E Publishers, 1984.

Rubin, Louis. *Facts and Feelings in the Classroom,* New York: Viking Press, 1973.

Tavris, Carol. *Anger: The Misunderstood Emotion,* New York: Viking Press, 1973.

Schrank, Jeffrey. *Teaching Human Beings,* Boston: Beacon Press, 1972.

Silberman, Chas. E. *Crisis in the Classroom,* New York: Vintage Books, 1971.

Weisinger, Hendrie. *Dr. Weisinger's Anger Workout Book,* New York: Quill Press, 1985.

Welsh, Patrick. *Tales Out of School,* New York: Viking Press, 1986.